CW01085946

Contents

Acknowledgements

Thanks to Darrell Burge for permission to use the Hornby, Airfix, Humbrol, Corgi and Scalextric adverts, Black Cat Firework Limited for use of the Standard Fireworks advert, Donna Bennett for the use of the Dinky and Matchbox adverts, Sacha da Cunha Soars for use of the Letraset Action Transfers advert and Kelda Roe and the Unilever archive for the use of the Walls and Brooke Bond adverts.

Thanks also to Flickr user 'Combom', Christopher Daniel and Alan Gold. A special thanks to Steve Barry who managed to recover lost text from a stubborn computer! Other photos and illustrations come from the Derek Tait Archive, Wikipedia and the American Library of Congress.

I have tried to track down all copyright holders of photos and illustrations used and apologise to anyone who hasn't been mentioned.

One

At Home

At the beginning of the 1960s, Harold Macmillan was the Prime Minister of Great Britain and Elizabeth II had been Queen since 1952. Popular television shows included Danger Man, starring Patrick McGoohan, Police Surgeon and ITV's first broadcasts of live Football League matches. Coronation Street made its debut on ITV on 9th December starting an intended 13 week run but has appeared on tv ever since.

Popular singing stars of the day include Adam Faith, Michael Holliday, Anthony Newley, Johnny Preston, Lonnie Donegan, The Everly Brothers, Elvis Presley and Cliff Richard.

At home, most families lived in rented accommodation, very few owned their own houses. There was no central heating, houses were draughty and most homes didn't have telephones. Many didn't have a television and the ones that did, rented them.

The 1960s were seen as a time of change. A time when the talk of war and rationing seemed a long way in the past.
For a boy born in the 1960s, life just seemed one big adventure. I was born in Plymouth in 1961 and my father was in the Navy and we very soon moved from Plymouth to Weymouth.
Our home had a black and white television and we definitely had a radio because I remember my parents listening to 'Downtown' by Petula Clark. That must have been in 1964.

At the local park in about 1962. All parks had concrete floors and usually had a concrete train or car to play on.

My early memories include being a very small boy, being in my push chair and my mum putting a jar of Robertson's Jam beside me, complete with golliwog, and I also recall feeding the swans at the harbour at Weymouth when I was about two. Lots of other memories from that time still stay in my head but are just simple things such as the postman and the milkman arriving in the morning and the excitement of riding upstairs on a double decker bus.

When you're a small child, everything seems amazing to you including postmen, milkmen, cars, buses, fire engines and ice cream vans. Everything is new, colourful and exciting.

In comparison to today, homes in the early 1960s were quite basic. There was no double glazing, no duvets and the only heating came from the modern gas or electric fire in the front room.

My brother and me shared a bedroom and pre-school days were filled with going to the shops with mum or going to the park. Alan was 5 year older than me so was at school all day while I was at home.

Winters seemed a lot colder in the 1960s and we'd always have home-knitted jumpers, scarves, balaclavas and mittens or gloves. All kids wore duffel coats complete with 'bear teeth' buttons. We liked to think at the time that they were real bear teeth but they were probably just made of plastic! In wet weather, we had our galoshes (a word you don't hear anymore, now replaced by 'Wellingtons') and would happily splash through endless puddles. There was always the smell of chimney smoke on cold days and evenings. Far more people had

This photo shows me in my pushchair on Guy Fawkes night in 1963 when I was just two years old. Yes, those are real monkeys and I remember well the time when one was put in my pushchair beside me!

coal fires back then and the air was often filled with smoke. I loved the smell!

There seemed to be more of everything back then including more birds, more insects, more post offices and more little shops. When you were a small boy in the 1960s, a trip to the grocer's or post office was an adventure. We all had our own toy shops with scaled down food packets and toy post offices with rubber stamps and envelopes.

We were certainly easier amused. While Alan was at school, mum would get my matchbox cars out and make me a circuit to drive them around out of wooden clothes pegs. That and colouring in kept me occupied all day. There was always Andy Pandy and Bill and Ben to watch on the television half way through the day. A trip to the shops was always an adventure but I would soon get fed up unless we were in the toyshop. I always hated going to the butchers with chopped up meat everywhere. There's no doubt that people ate a lot more meat back then but I was never keen even as a boy!

Going to school was a big change in any kid's life. Instead of hanging around with your mother all day, playing and enjoying yourself, you suddenly found yourself in a classroom of 40 other kids that you probably didn't know. It was a daunting experience for a small boy although all we ever did was a bit of counting, learning to tell the time and painting although, after being at home all day, it all suddenly seemed a bit intimidating - a feeling that stayed with me all through school!

Sat on the harbour at Weymouth, aged 2, happily feeding the swans. I can still remember that day!

We loved visiting my gran and great aunties and uncles who lived in Seaham Harbour in Durham. It seemed a lot colder there and the snow would be right up against the door which I loved. We were so pleased to see it that, in between having snow ball fights and building snowmen, we quite happily cleared all the old folks drives nearby. One of them had fought in the First World War and gladly showed me all of his medals. My Aunt Nan always had lots of cats when we visited her and would always buy us the latest games and toys. I remember two games she bought me - *Mount Everest* and *Tippet* which I loved! Aunt Hannah would read our tea leaves (we made sure she gave us her tea cards!) and would tell our fortunes as well as tell us of the various ghosts she'd seen. It seemed very cold in the North then and I loved lying in front of gran's coal fire watching the flames and listening to it crackle. I was also fascinated that they got different programmes to the ones we got in the South and we'd watch shows like *Time Tunnel* on her ghosty rental black and white television. We never could get a good picture on it and we'd be holding the table top aerial all around the room trying to get a better picture. I'm sure the rental shop saw her off. At night, being small, my bed would be two armchairs pushed together and I'd fall asleep with the coal fire still crackling listening to my gran's old clock ticking away. It chimed every quarter of an hour but we had to turn in off because it kept us awake all night.

In the day, if we weren't visiting relatives, Alan and me would explore the nearby shops. They were different to ours in Plymouth. Nowadays, all shops, wherever you go, seem all much the same. I remember one day was so cold and blustery that, as we were returning to gran's, I was lifted off my feet by the wind.

In 1968, we moved into a naval flat at Devonport. Alan and me had a bedroom upstairs in the flat and we could see everyone going by from the window. There seemed allsorts to do and we were always out playing. Alan had a book that showed you how to make things such as a telephone out of two tins and a piece of string. We tried it but it didn't seem to work very good.

For a while, in the summer, we had a dog called Bambi. He was a brown Spaniel. However, a flat was too small to keep a dog and dad was at work and we were at school so he was soon given away. I remember Alan and me searching for him the next day but we never saw him again. Mum decided to buy us a blue budgie instead which we called Fred. He was lovely and very tame and lived with us for the rest of the time we lived at Devonport. He'd happily fly around the front room and was quite tame.

Across from where we lived was a newsagents. I loved going there mainly for sweets and American comics. Mum got to know the owner, Mrs Crook, and she said that we could stay in her caravan for a few days. We were all very excited. The caravan was at Challaborough and was very old. I loved it though! It was so old that it still had gas lamps. It rained most of the time but when it was dry, Alan and me would go out exploring and one day we ended up at Bigbury where there was a huge arcade which included slot machines and dodgem cars. We loved it! Alan put a penny in one machine and said for me to look into it. It was an old 'What the Butler Saw' machine and the pictures inside were all pretty tame just old drawings and paintings of women in their underwear. After we'd played all the machines, we were wandering back to the caravan and I was worried and kept saying to Alan, 'Don't tell mum that we looked at the What the Butler Saw machine!'.

In the end, it rained so much and the caravan leaked so much that we headed off back home. It had seemed a great adventure to me though.

A selection of Captain Scarlet badges which were given away free with breakfast cereal. The large badge was bought by my gran on one of her visits to Plymouth.

During the summer holidays, my gran came down to stay with us from her home in Seaham Harbour. We loved seeing her and she would take us to the pictures in town and buy us sweets and other things. Captain Scarlet was on the telly which all kids loved and gran bought me a Captain Scarlet badge which I wore all summer (I've still got it). We all loved collecting bubblegum cards and gran would buy us some. All the kids were collecting Captain

We all loved to collect bubblegum cards and the ones shown here were the most sought after. They include cards from The Champions, Superman, Land of the Giants, The Man from Uncle, Tarzan and, of course, Captain Scarlet.

Scarlet cards so there were wrappers from the bubblegum everywhere. There was an offer that if you collected 40 wrappers you could send away for a Captain Scarlet poster so we collected up all the discarded wrappers and sent them off. We loved the poster when it came and it was stuck up on our bedroom wall.

For a while, everything we bought had Captain Scarlet on it including breakfast cereal, ice lollies, sweet cigarette cards, bubblegum cards, badges and toys. At night, we would shine a torch on the bedroom ceiling and say in our deepest voices, 'WE ARE THE MYSTERONS!'.

Some kids really did believe they were indestructible, like Captain Scarlet, and would jump off high walls and garages. Most landed uninjured (some copied commando rolls that they'd seen on the telly or in films). Occasionally, one would break his arm and injure himself and then we all thought that we were in for trouble.

Most of our summer holidays were spent exploring the area. There were no good places to build dens (my den building days would start at our next house) so we would go to the nearest park and play. The park would be considered dangerous nowadays with its concrete floor. There were a few swings, a slide and a seesaw as well as a few concrete pipes for kids to play in. The pipes always smelled of urine so nobody spent anytime in there. I remember being pleased that I found a Captain Black bubblegum card in there, another one for my Captain Scarlet collection!

Sometimes we would have a picnic in the park, usually banana sandwiches, and we'd climb up onto the old concrete shelters there and wave back to our mum at home. I remember one picnic that we had in the park where a seagull pooped straight into my cup of tomato soup! That put me off tomato soup for ages.

You don't see kids doing it nowadays but we would all roll on our sides from the top of the grassy hill by the park to the bottom. Many would lose their pocket money on the journey down but usually found someone else's before they went home. That bank must be littered with old coins nowadays.

There were other kids in the flats so we played with them. One of the kids, a girl, had a big white dog called Kim. The dog was so big that she let all the kids have a ride on it! Amazingly, the dog didn't mind. We'd also take our toys out into the street and play. We had some battery operated tin robots, that we'd brought back from our time in Singapore, that the other kids were amazed with. The robots talked, walked and fired guns.

We all had a collection of Timpo cowboys and soldiers and we'd sometimes have mock battles with those.

A classic Horikawa battery operated tin robot which walked, spun around and fired machine guns from its chest.

Other kids would have butterfly nets and go out hunting for different species. Amazingly, the area was quite built up but there were still hundreds of more butterflies and insects than there are nowadays. One boy in the flats would catch butterflies, kill them and pin them to a board. That's something we would never do and I remember that he got annoyed when we released all the butterflies he'd caught that day so that he wouldn't be able to kill them. There were so many about that he probably soon caught some more!

Insects like butterflies, ladybirds, bees and wasps were far more in abundance in those days than they are today. Even away from any greenery, there seemed to be many varieties of butterflies. It wasn't unusual for someone to come home crying who had been stung by a bee or a wasp as they were everywhere.

There would always be something to do. We'd often run through the corridors of the flats either pretending to be Napoleon Solo and Illya Kuryakin or the characters from *Time Tunnel* or *Lost in Space*.

The only thing that would interrupt our playing was our mums calling us in for our tea.

The chimes of the ice cream van would have us all running to our mums to get change for an ice lolly which usually came with a free card or badge. We all looked forward to the ice cream van visiting so that we could get our favourite lollies which included free picture cards which, in the 1960s, usually had something to do with

A Walls Sky Ray Moon Fleet badge given away with ice lollies.

outer space.

There was always a fete or fair on during the summer and we'd end up at most of them. I remember going to one and there was a raffle and we seemed to win most of the prizes!

Being near to the dockyard, we also went to Navy Days and had a great time. There were lots of activities for the kids including games organised by sailors dressed as pirates. Dad knew many of the people on the base so we had our dinner aboard one of the ships. It seemed a great adventure to us.

We spent all summer playing out of doors as most kids did back then. We got into some scrapes but always seemed to have a great time.

In the evenings, even in the winter, we'd wander down to the Aggie Weston Sailors' Rest building. Outside, illuminated in a glass case, was a large bible which would be open on different pages. We'd go down there just to see if the page had been turned over which showed how easily amused we were!

A selection of cards that were given away free with Lyons Maid
and Walls Ice lollies. They included space cards, pop stars,
inventors and Doctor Who.

Lots of kids would re-enact things they'd seen on the telly
so there would be kids pretending to be Captain Scarlet
or Orlando O'Connor (a long since forgotten series
starring Sam Kydd). Patrick Troughton was Doctor Who
at the time, which everyone loved. It gave me nightmares
though especially the episodes with the Daleks and the
Cyberman. Alan and me would run through the corridors.
He'd be Doctor Who and I'd be chasing him as either a

A collection of Lyons Maid 'Galaxy Patrol' badges. They were obtained by collecting tokens from Lyons Maid ice lollies and sending them away to receive a badge of your choice.

Dalek, Cyberman or Yeti until we were called in for our tea. There were great cards you could collect from Wall's Ice cream featuring Doctor Who and we had most of them. Every day in the summer, the ice cream van would come around. We'd all listen out for the tunes it played as it approached including *Popeye the Sailorman*, *Greensleeves* and *Raindrops keep falling on your head*. Many of the ice lollies came with free cards which included a set called Space Age Britain. There was also a series of badges called Galaxy Patrol which you could send away for by collecting the tokens from special wrappers. You could also send away for wallcharts to stick your cards on and we had one on our bedroom wall. Kids loved collecting things. Apart from bubblegum cards, there were also cards given away with boxes of Brooke Bond tea (no teabags back then!). We all had albums which included cards of cars, famous costumes, flags and animals. We all made sure that we got our

Four Robertson's Golliwog statues which were obtained by sending one shilling and tokens from Robertson's jam. The whole set included a guitar player, an accordion player, a clarinet player, a drummer, an oboe player and a singer. An additional, and rarer statue, featured a lollipop man.

A badge given away with Brooke Bond tea.

mums to buy Robertson's jam so we could collect the golliwog tokens and send off for a golliwog statue or badge. I think you also had to send a shilling as well to cover postage. I remember ours arriving in a small box with the golliwog and a lot of straw. He was put in the display cabinet in the front room but dad knocked him off and he was decapitated (the golliwog, that is!). A bit of glue soon fixed him.

There was always something you could win on chocolate or other food. I remember Alan being out and I was bored so mum got me to colour in the Magic Roundabout picture on the back of the Instant Whip packet. She sent it in and I won a Magic Roundabout colouring set which I thought was great at the time. Alan and me also did a competition to win a Dalek and we imagined climbing inside and driving it around the estate. We didn't win it but it was fun thinking that we might.

Mum would take me to school and I remember autumn days kicking all the leaves up as we made our way there. The school had regular jumble sales and I remember I had a collection of Rupert annuals bought there which I loved.

We loved Halloween and the lead up to Bonfire night.

A pound note from the 1960s. It was worth much more than it would be today and most boys wouldn't have had one. Most had a few coppers and perhaps a threepence in their pockets!

Mum would carve us lanterns out of turnips (in the same way they do with pumpkins today). There was no trick or treating back then but just being out on the streets carrying a lantern at that time of year, would bring in a few pennies from passersby. I remember one evening in 1968 and mum and dad had gone to a party and we were being looked after by our next door neighbour. We took our lanterns out to see if we could make some money. A bloke, who must have been in his twenties, came up to us and started talking to us. He had a few friends with him and they started chatting to us. I always remember that his name was 'Derek' the same as mine. Anyhow, suddenly he produced a machete, chopped my brother's turnip in four and all three men fled with my turnip. Alan and me ran all the way home, crying. We told our neighbour who told our mum and dad. Nowadays, if such a thing happened, the police would be called, there would be a manhunt and it would be the headlines in the local paper. Back then, everything was soon forgotten and we were soon making a guy to take out to ask passersby, 'Penny for the Guy'! Alan had the bright idea to set our guy up outside the nearest pub. It went well and we got lots of pennies but then when we said to one bloke, 'Penny for the Guy', he gave us a penny and took the guy in the pub! He came out about ten minutes later, laughing, and gave us back our guy and two shillings, which was a fortune to us back then.

The next night, Alan decided we could make a lot better guy if we just put a mask on him and pretended he was a dummy. All went well for a while until some bloke came up and punched him in the face! He was only 12 at the time and I was 7. Even with everything that went on, we still enjoyed ourselves and were happy with the money we made.

Fireworks night involved a few rockets set off by dad from a milk bottle and a few sparklers. The rougher kids would buy bangers and chuck them at unsuspecting passersby!

We entered this competition to win a full-size Dalek but didn't win (which was probably just as well!). Many years later, I built my own.

There were lots of adverts on the telly warning of the dangers of throwing fireworks at people (which didn't seem to stop some kids!).

We all loved firework night and would pester are parents to buy us as many as possible. Rockets and sparklers were our favourites.

Fireworks were only ever set off on 5th November and we'd get dad to buy us some. In those days, they consisted mainly of rockets (shot from a milk bottle), sparklers, Catherine Wheels and Roman Candles. Sometimes there would be an organised firework display and we'd go to that. Kids had their own bonfires everywhere ready to set on fire (with their guy on top) on Guy Fawkes night. Some were an incredible size. Inevitably, other kids would always set fire to them early which we'd miss because we were always at school the week leading up to 5th November. If your fire did survive, it was great fun gathering around it, waving sparklers and breathing in the smoke. Our clothes would stink of it afterwards and later, when we were tucked up in bed, I could still see the flickering of the flames when I closed my eyes.

Towards Christmas, Alan's class at school put on a pantomime and we all went along to see it. We all enjoyed shouting out phrases like, 'He's behind you!'. By the end of the year, we were ready to leave our flat and move to our new house which was further out of town.

I remember the first time we went to see the new house. It was on the outskirts of the city so mum took me on the bus to have a look at it. I was 7 at the time. I was amazed when we arrived there because a squirrel ran across the path in front of us. Neither of us had ever seen one before. Nowadays, they're absolutely everywhere but back then it was very rare to see one. I loved our new street. Some houses were still being built and there was a

The change that you could expect to find in your pocket during the 1960s including a farthing, a halfpenny, a penny, a threepence, a sixpence, a shilling, two shillings and a half crown. Farthings were legal tender until 1960 and halfcrowns were withdrawn in 1967. They were a lot heavier than modern coins and consequently led to holes in your pockets!

building site at the end of the street would looked a great place for a boy to play - lots of walls to climb and building materials left around everywhere. Ideal for making dens in the nearby woods. The house was backed

32

by woods with more trees in front and my new school just in front of that. To me it was just like being out in the country and that's what I told everyone back at school. The house still had bare floors and needed finishing but looked great to me. Upstairs, Alan and me had our own bedroom overlooking the woods.

There's one other reason why I remember the day that we visited our new house in 1968. On the way back, we caught the bus again and I made sure we sat upstairs. When it was coming to our stop and we were waiting by the doors, someone rang the bell and the doors flew open and I fell off the bus. Luckily, I'd grabbed the bar that stood beside the door and hung onto it tight as my legs flew in the air as the bus continued to move. The conductor saw what was happening and quickly jumped out of the front door of the bus and caught me. I could have easily been killed if not for the quick actions of the conductor and I remember my mum crying when we got back to the flat.

At the beginning of 1969, we left for our new house and Alan and me were soon settled into our new bedroom, complete with bunk beds. Alan had the top one and I had the bottom one.

He'd sometimes tell me stories at bedtime, he made them up as he went along, and they would always end with mum shouting, 'Go to sleep!'

It's hard to imagine the dawn chorus nowadays as all the birds in the woods woke up at about 5am in the morning. There were far more birds around then than there are nowadays and it was incredible to hear.

Every morning the milkman and postman would arrive very early in the morning, certainly before mum and dad set off for work and before we'd set off for school. You could set your watch by them. Quite often the silver tops on top of the milk bottles would be pecked by Blue Tits. It's odd that they learned how to do this and birds up and down the country all did the same thing. We loved Gold Top which was thick and creamy. Although we never ordered it, the milkman would sometimes accidentally leave it. It was great on cornflakes (with lots of sugar!). Milk always came in bottles back then and there were no cardboard cartons and definitely no skimmed or semi-skimmed milk.

The builders of our new house didn't put the back fence up for ages and some mornings, we would wake up and there would be cows in the back garden. I wish I had a photo! It wasn't unusual to see a cow walking along past the front door. There were many farms around back then but today, it's hard to imagine as they've all been replaced with housing estates.

We soon made friends with the other new kids in the street and we were all soon visiting and playing on the building site at the end of the street. Everything was just left lying around so was handy for taking off into the woods to make dens. There were always plenty of sheets of corrugated iron which were excellent to use as walls. Every day the builders came in for work in the mornings, they must have wondered what had gone on the evening before. We'd be down there straight after school, lining up bottles on the walls and smashing them with home-made catapults, playing in the half-built houses, jumping off banks pretending to be Batman and carting off anything we could to make dens or go-karts. In those day, kids had a pretty much free reign to do what they wanted and as soon as they had their tea after school, they were straight out again.

We loved it when it snowed. We had one I-Spy book which featured animal tracks and I remember Alan and me setting off early one morning after it had snowed to look for the imprints of weird and wonderful animals and birds.

I'm sure that we probably thought that we'd discovered tracks of deer, foxes, badgers and other wild animals but the prints probably just belonged to the local cats and dogs. It was all very exciting though and we were spurred on by watching shows like Scooby Doo and reading Enid Blyton books. I even thought that we might come across the footprints of a Yeti which seemed to appear in a lot of kids cartoons where there was snow! When we didn't find any prints we just left our own which were made by putting four fingers together and pushing them in the snow to look like wild cats. We even left big Yeti footprints which I'm sure fooled no-one!

Wayfinders brought out excellent shoes at the time that all the kids had to have. The sole featured various animal pawprints, which you could leave in the snow, and in the heel was a compass. Nobody ever used the compass to find their way home but we'd all seen people do similar things on the telly and it somehow seemed adventurous. Tuf shoes were also out at the same time but always gave you blisters. Clark's shoes were Tuf's rivals and were a lot more comfortable. Every boy wanted a pair of Clark's Commandos!

We played out so much that most of us never had much time to do any school homework and I'm sure that most of us were told off for it by the teachers the next day.

Our dens were fantastic. They were all built in the woods. Some went underground and some were built into the many old air-raid shelters that still stood amongst the woods. Some of our dens were quite elaborate - one had two armchairs in it that we found lying around! I remember finding one and Alan pushing me in it down the pavement to our den. We were having great fun until one miserable old bloke came out of his house and told us off for 'scratching the pavement!'. On school days, you always wanted to get back home and out quickly to check how your den was. There was always other groups of kids from other estates on the look out for dens to wreck and that's usually what happened to most of them.

At the time, there were lots of spy shows on the tv so we all made up names for ourselves so if the police came along (which never happened) and asked us what we were up to, we could give them a false name. We pinned our assumed names up in our posh den (the one with the armchairs). I can't remember anyone else's name but my own. For some reason, I called myself 'Peter Swindler'! I remember mum finding the list and saying, 'Who's Peter Swindler?

There was a man who always showed up when the kids were out playing. Some of the kids would know him and he would run around pretending to machine-gun any flies that were about. Someone said that a bomb had landed on his house during the war which had affected him. I think that most kids found it all pretty scary.

Kids used to build things back then and many would make their own go-karts. There were always bit of wood and old pram wheels to hand and some kids (and their dads probably) turned out some great go-karts. If someone turned up on one while we were playing, we could spend the rest of the day taking turns on it.

Alan used to like making bikes, there were always old ones thrown in the nearby creek so he'd make a couple of decent ones out of all the bits. I remember Alan teaching me how to ride it which involved him sitting on the back and steering but jumping off once we were going without telling me! It seemed to work as I was soon riding it on my own.

We both had one of Alan's homemade bikes but being only 7 at the time, my feet wouldn't touch the ground so I had to fall off it when I wanted to get off. I'd always go home with huge bruises on my legs because of this. I also had many near misses and scrapes on the bike but the worst was when we were riding down a steep concrete path. I left the path to avoid a little girl who had walked onto it but as I went back on the path, my wheel caught the verge and I flew off landing directly on my head. Alan took me home crying and dad took me straight up the A&E. I had a big bruise on my head for weeks afterwards and I remember a girl at school kept asking to see it. I've still got the lump today!

Sometimes, if Alan and me were up early in the holidays

Every boy wanted a Corgi Batmobile for their birthday or Christmas!

38

or on a Saturday, we would catch the milkman and buy a pint of milk off him and drink it while we sat in the sunshine on the roofs of the nearby garages. The reason that we were on the garages was that we'd jump off the end pretending to be commandos. Occasionally, someone would come out and tell us off but it didn't happen very much because in those days everyone was at work. There seems to be a lot more people at home nowadays. After we'd played on the garages for a while we'd go to the nearby block of flats just to ride up and down in the lifts. It sounds crazy today but back then lifts were relatively new and there were many kids that had never been in one!

Alan had a paper round that seemed to go on for miles. I can't remember how much he got paid a week but it didn't seem much. Sometimes, I would go with him and give him a hand. He would give me a 'backy' on his push bike and we'd race between one address and another, I remember that there was a very steep hill with just a few people who got the paper down at the bottom. We used to travel down that hill as fast as Alan's bike would go with me hanging on precariously on the back. I remember that there was one old man on the round who would always moan that his paper was late, even if it was early! Alan did well for tips at Christmas, apart from the moany old bloke! I can't remember what he spent it all on although I do remember going to the local sweet shop some nights and buying chocolate mice, milk bottles and flying saucers (all types of sweets).

Every so often, we'd be taken to the local barber. Ours was above the local fish and chip shop. The barber only did one haircut for boys which meant you ended up with it completely sheared! Going to school the next day was always embarrassing and most kids would keep their duffle coat hoods up as much as possible. Some smart kid would always creep up behind you and pull your hood down and shout, 'He's had his hair cut!'. The teacher would even notice and point it out to the whole class. Luckily, it grew back eventually!

It was quite uncommon for houses to have phones at the time and most people went out to the many phone boxes that were around to make a phone call. When we first got a phone, it seemed amazing and we all kept staring at it. Mum would always put on her phone voice when answering it. When it was first fitted, it just picked up Radio One and nothing else. I don't know how this was possible but the engineer soon came back and fixed it. We were amazed just by dialling up the speaking clock! There was another service called, 'Dial-A-Disc' where you could dial 16 and listen to the latest chart hits. You couldn't imagine anyone doing it nowadays but back then it was the equivalent of looking up your favourite song on YouTube today. There were other phone services offered by the then GPO. These included the cricket results. All the phones had old fashioned dials but even so, they seemed very modern in those days. Also, compared to today's phones, they were very heavy.

Outdoors, we'd make our own bows and arrows and fire at targets (they were never very good) and make catapults for firing at tin cans. There were plenty of squirrels and

Corgi Rockets were excellent and we'd have tracks spread across our bedroom so the cars could speed from one end to the other doing a loop-de-loop on the way!

41

pigeons around but we would have never have aimed our catapults at them. Most kids loved animals although there was always the odd idiot about who should have known better! We also all had water pistols, which were great in the long hot summers, and spud guns (which fired bits of potato at your friends!) and toy machine guns and cowboy pistols, complete with paper caps, for when we were fighting battles.

I remember one wonderful sunny summer's day when all the kids in the area met up to build a combined den in the woods. It didn't come to much and I remember spending most of the day lying in the ferns, taking it easy, staring up at the blue sky. The smell of ferns still reminds me of my childhood. The den didn't come to much and there was a fight at the end of it all between the other kids but I can't remember what it was about. Anyhow, that den was soon abandoned.

A kid, who lived along the street, and me found a fence panel one day and made a great den in the woods with it. We camouflaged it with ferns so that no-one could see it, it was excellent. Later that day, we returned and Alan and a friend were taking it apart. He said that they hadn't wrecked it but we had our doubts. Getting your den destroyed seemed to happen often. That's probably what the earlier fight was about!

We had a tent and sometimes Alan and me would camp in the back garden. We'd sleep out all night. Usually, we'd be talking so much or laughing that mum would end up shouting out of the window for us to go to sleep.

I remember that if it rained and one of us touched the canvas, it would leak all night. Sometimes in the summer, I used to sit in the tent reading books. It was sort of like having a ready made den.

Alan would build his own bikes from bits and pieces that he would find. We both had one but my legs would never quite touch the ground. Alan taught me how to ride a bike on one of these on the nearby field at the end of the road. He would sit on the back steering and then jump off leaving me to ride it. To start off, I would wobble a bit and then fall off. Because I was too small for the bike, I would end up with huge bruises on the inside of my legs. I soon got the hang of it and very soon we were riding as fast as we could down the long, steep concrete path that ran beside the nearby football pitches. It was great fun until one day, a man and his little girl were walking towards me on the path. I was going to fast to stop so I went around them and came back onto the path. As I did, I flew off the bike and landed hard on the concrete path, straight on my head, nearly knocking myself out. I was crying and a huge bump came up. The man walking his daughter wasn't the slightest bit interested and Alan took me home and then mum and dad rushed me up to the hospital. Once I was examined, they let me go back home but my head looked like it belonged to Frankenstein and it seemed like I had a bruised head for weeks after that. I've still got the bump! I'm not sure how long it was before I got on a bike again after that!

I would spend hours before we had Shep (I got him later in the 1970s for passing my 11+) looking through the pages of the Observer book of dogs trying to decide which dog that I'd most like to have. The ones that I picked were nearly always a variation of Lassie who was on the tv all of the time.

The varieties of dogs back then were totally different to the ones today. There were no Rottweilers, Staffordshire Bull Terriers or many of the other scarier breeds that you get nowadays. The common dogs then were Corgis, Alsatians, Poodles, Collies, Dachshunds and Labradors. There were certainly plenty of mongrels because many dogs just roamed the streets. I can't remember any kid that I knew ever getting attacked by a wandering dog but I suppose that it must have happened. The scary dog that every kid feared back then was the Alsatian, maybe because police dog handlers used them. There used to be a police dog handler who lived close to us on the way to the shops. He would keep his dog in a big cage in the garden. The cage was about 6 ft tall so the top of it overlooked the wall that surrounded the house. As kids, we would put our hands, flat on top of the wall and the second that we did, the dog would go crazy. We'd than run off! We all hoped that we wouldn't meet the dog out on the streets somewhere but occasionally, we would come across him with his handler. The dog would come after you too but, luckily, he was well trained and would stop as soon as the handler told him too. Sometimes, it all seemed a bit too close for comfort! My mum was coming home from the shop one day, cutting through the school on her way back when the Alsatian came after her. 'Stay where you are!', shouted the handler, to which my mum replied, 'Do you mean me or the dog?'.

Some days, we would go to the local zoo. Mum and dad would take us sometimes and sometimes Alan and me just went on our own. I think it was a shilling to get in. It was only a very tiny zoo but contained chimps, seals, polar bears, giraffes, a hippo and lions etc. I remember the first time that we all went as a family and a pelican followed us all the way around. It was like he was making sure that we saw everything! At the beginning of the zoo, you could buy sweet popcorn which was meant for the animals. It was the first time that I'd ever tasted sweet popcorn and we probably ate most of it ourselves. I'm sure that it wouldn't have done the animals any good anyway! I remember one time when a giraffe snatched the empty bag from our hand and was just going to swallow it. We thought that it would choke but luckily, we managed to get it back!

The shop in the zoo sold all sorts of souvenirs including badges, pendants and chimpanzee masks. I bought a chimpanzee mask and wore it all the way home on the bus. The conductor didn't even comment. As we were getting back home, we saw our neighbours who were moving out. I still had my chimp's mask on and the neighbour just shook my hand and said, 'Goodbye, Derek!' as they set off to leave. Nobody mentioned the mask. Of course, I had to take it off when it came to tea time!

We all enjoyed collecting things which included cereal toys, bubblegum cards, coins, keys and badges. One thing that most children seemed to have a collection of was stamps. We all had our own albums and you could

Nellie the elephant at the local zoo. A similar elephant stole the umbrella of our teacher, Mr Smith!

join a stamp club in various comics to get more stamps. With dad being in the Navy, Alan and me had a huge collection from all over the world. I would love to have them all today but they seemed to disappear sometime in the 1970s. I can't imagine kids collecting stamps nowadays.

For a while, every boy seemed to be in the Cubs and every girl seemed to be in the Brownies. I joined up and nagged my mum to buy me the uniform. She wouldn't because she said I would soon be bored with it. Other

Some badges that I collected at Plymouth Zoo during the 1960s. I'm glad that I kept them, unfortunately, my chimp mask disappeared a long time ago!

kids didn't get their whole uniform at once either. People didn't have the money back then. One week they'd have their scarf and toggle, the next week they'd get their shorts, then their shirt and so on. Anyway, mum was right, I soon got fed up with it and left! I didn't even get my toggle but managed to stay for about 6 weeks. If there was a badge for losing interest, I'd have got it. Thinking back now, it was good fun and we did a bit of orienteering (just in the local woods). I never did understand compasses!

Birds eggs were another thing that boys collected, although I never did. An egg would be taken from a nest, poked with a pin at each end, and the inside blown out before the egg was displayed. Hobbies and outdoor interests were encouraged by books, parents and schools. We'd quite happily go off into the woods to collect various different leaves for a school project or track down and observe wildlife. Every activity seemed to involve being outdoors.

Home life certainly changed from the beginning of the 1960s until the end of the decade. Homes had more luxury, gadgets, heating and were more brightly decorated. Many people owned their own homes and many had a car and television set.

There'll never be another decade like the 1960s; great television, the best toys ever, wild fashions and a childhood full of fun, playing out in the sunshine until our mothers called us in for tea.

Two

School

For many, school in the 1960s wasn't a pleasant experience and far detached from the way of teaching nowadays. Teachers could be strict, were allowed to beat you if they felt like it, pull your ear or hair or shake you around. There's no doubt that many of the teachers if transported straight from the 1960s to nowadays would be instantly arrested! Everyone who went to school in the 1960s will remember at least one teacher who looked like his blood was ready to boil who would fly off the handle on any occasion. There were teachers you just didn't mess with and in whose classes you were always well behaved. There's no doubt that many of the teachers of the 1960s weren't suited to their profession, didn't like children at all and were in many ways unbalanced.

Every child who went to school in the 1960s will have at least one tale of a teacher who was either too heavy with his hands or the cane. Many children will also remember senior teachers who almost seemed like they were from another world. They certainly weren't like our parents. We later had one teacher who reminded me of Ronnie Kray. The only difference was that Ronnie Kray smiled occasionally!

When we returned to England from Singapore, my first school was temporary. We lived in a Naval flat which I loved. My new school was in a Victorian building which had seen better days. The infants were taught in huts detached from the main building and later at a separate annexe away from the school.

I was 6 years old at the time so was still in the infants. We all had our own little leather satchels that contained our exercise book, a pencil (we weren't allowed to use pens until we were 11!), a snack for break time and a drink. Lessons consisted of basic things like telling the time properly, spelling, maths and a bit of geography. I remember the teacher getting annoyed because no-one knew the difference between a county and a country. If only she'd bothered to explain it! We also did a lot of craft work including cutting out bits of cloth and making pictures (the scissors were always incredibly blunt) and painting, which I loved. We always took the pictures home to show our mums! There was also the dreaded PE where we ran around a bit, did some forward rolls, and then had a bit of a sleep. I was at the school long enough to have a change of teachers. Our new teacher must have been about twenty and I remember she had jet black hair. She wasn't the most calmest of people and was forever shouting at her class and we often would have to sit quietly with our hands on our heads. I remember that there was one kid who was always naughty and one day he decided that he would flood the classroom by putting

My school report from Christmas 1968. For once, I was above average (it didn't last!). The slip on the bottom was meant to be signed by your parents and returned but. by the following term, we'd moved to a new house and I was at a new school.

the plugs in the sink and leaving the taps on as we were all going home. I remember the teacher catching him, pulling his pants down and giving him a good spanking! It was a different world back then and I doubt his parents even complained but even as a 6 year old I thought it was a bit much. All the girls in the class talked about it for weeks.

I saw a different side to my teacher one day though. We were transferred to the annexe but no-one had told my mum so there was no-one to pick me up when I left school. She saw that I was lost and walked me all the way home and was absolutely lovely! I suppose she just couldn't cope with some of the unruly kids in the class and it was all a bit much for her. I even felt sorry for her when she got me back to our flat and my parents told her off because they didn't know where I was. I was soon settled down and watching the telly and I had soon forgotten about being worried that no-one met me. I drive past the same place nowadays. The school is long gone but it still brings back memories of that day.

By the time I attended the school it was already pretty run down and most of the lessons were taken in added on huts. In the morning, during lessons, someone would be nominated to be the milk monitor and would hand out bottles of milk to all the class complete with a straw. The bottles were a third of a pint and we were given them all through the infants and juniors. The main part of the building housed the classroom for the older kids as well as the assembly hall. All the schools trophies were housed there too. There was a black and white television

All boys loved things that could fly like toy discs and planes. In class, we'd make paper aeroplanes and throw them about while the teacher was writing on the blackboard!

to watch programmes for schools which did their best to inform pupils about maths, reading and geography. There was one adventure series that was on every week that I loved and it was a very Enid Blyton-like story with lots of mystery and clues. We had booklets that we all had to answer questions about the show. Our teacher decided in the art part of our class that we would paint the characters from the show and our part of the class had to paint one of the baddies. I remember the other kids moaning when I started to paint his suit blue. It seemed unheard of in the 1960s that anyone would have a suit any other colour than black!

Every dinnertime, we had to trail off to another school to get our school dinner. It was quite a way away and we'd all walk there holding hands. Before we set off, the teacher would make sure we'd all been to the toilet. The toilets were smelly falling-down horrible places and I remember one day that even though I was bursting, I couldn't go with another kid standing next to me so I hung onto it. By the time we all got to the other school, I could hold onto it no longer. One of the dinner ladies let me use their toilet but it was too late. When I got back to the dinner table, one of the older boys who was serving out the food said to me, 'Spotted Dick?' which he thought was hilarious.

There was a school bully who looked something like a baboon. He was older than me but I was never sure if he went to the school or just turned up on occasions and wandered in. Anyway, when we got back to school the same day, he'd already heard about the incident at dinner

KNOWLE   PRIMARY   SCHOOL,   PLYMOUTH

REPORT for .....*Summer*...................... Term, 19 *6.9*...

NAME .....*Derek John*.................. YEAR OF JUNIOR COURSE................

NUMBER IN CLASS ....*38*.................. PUNCTUALITY ....*Very Good*...........

SUBJECTS		GRADE*	COMMENTS
ENGLISH	Reading	5	*Derek's reading has improved and most of this is now done with confidence at moving along.*
	Comprehension		
	Language Study		
	Composition	4	*Some of his imaginative work has been good.*
	Spelling		
ARITHMETIC 1 (Basic Skills)		5	*Needs more practice in the multiplication.*
ARITHMETIC 2 (Application of skills and general Mathematics)			*However his work on graphs shows signs of progress.*
HISTORY			*He answers questions to gain good study skill experience,*
GEOGRAPHY			*although still rather elementary.*
SCIENCE			
SKILLS (Craft, art, handwriting Needlework—girls)			*His handwriting is good although it is poor.*
* GRADING Grading is done on a seven point scale. Grade 1 represents outstanding ability. Grade 4 is the standard achieved by an average child			*With greater care however he could write more quickly for handling his pictures.*

PHYSICAL ACTIVITY .... OUT OF SCHOOL ACTIVITIES..................

HOMEWORK ....*done*.....*generally*......

GENERAL REMARKS *A good term's work for his mixed work in the most work and always works quickly and well. A conscientious boy and a helpful member of the form. A delightful child to teach.*

An encouraging start.

Continued overleaf if necessary

.....*W. Hextree*.....Class Master/Mistress   *Blake*.....Head Master

---

A school report from the summer of 1969. A grade of '4' was average but I notice that I had two '5's' ! Even still, the headmaster wrote 'an encouraging start'. Perhaps he didn't even read it.

and said to me, 'I heard you peed yourself!'. He was a pain in the backside but never bothered me much. I think he might have been expelled and just turned up sometimes for no other reason than he was bored.

Boys and girls were taught in the same class but once it was playtime, we had our own separate playgrounds and there'd be trouble if a boy strayed into the girls playground. We were only 6 at the time so I don't know what they thought was going to happen. There was always the threat of the cane and having to see the headmaster so no-one broke the rules. Only the naughty kid would dare venture over the line. He got up to allsorts, including the flooding incident, and had to see the headmaster many times. The headmaster was miserable looking with a mop of black hair. Today, I remember him looking something like the MP, Gordon Brown. His son attended the school and I once had a fight with him right under the headmaster's office. I thought that I was bound to be in trouble when he leaned out of his window on the top floor but he just shooed us off. I think that was my only encounter with him.

Apart from painting, we also made paper mache saucers. We had to bring a saucer from home and cover it with papier-mâché which once dry, we'd paint and then they'd be left outside to dry in the sun. I couldn't have been very artistic at the time because I just painted mine brown! I still took it home, together with all my paintings, for my mum.

I found a couple of my old school reports and lessons included reading, writing, story writing or composition,

All kids loved Action Transfers which could be rubbed down onto cardboard adventure scenes (we were easily amused!). Popular characters included astronauts, soldiers, cars, Tarzan and favourite cartoon characters.

sums or scoring games, everyday or practical arithmetic, creative art and PE or games. In December 1968, I'd have been 7 years old and I see that I got 87 out of 100 in my maths test which was probably as good as it was ever going to get! In the story writing section, it says : 'Derek is capable of writing several sentences on his own and expressing his own news'.

Christmas was a lovely time at school and we'd all make decorations mainly chains made out of coloured paper. We'd also make Christmas cards for our parents

There was also the school nativity play to look forward to. Everyone would get there mum's to make them costumes and we'd play the parts of the three wise men, Joseph and Mary etc. I remember there was one swotty kid in class who always had to be better than everyone else. While the rest of the class turned up with white sheets and a towel with a belt on their heads for a costume, he turned up looking like he'd just appeared in the theatre.

Once Christmas was over, we were soon on the move to our new house and a new school. I told everyone it was out in the country, it seemed a long way away to me, but actually it was just further out of the city. Oddly, I dreamt about my new school the day before I went there and when I got there, it was exactly the same.

It was newer than my old school and had only stood for about 10 years although there was a fort surrounding it which was much older.

I was still in the infants when I got to the new school. Our house was right near to the school so I could get up later, have my breakfast, get washed and dressed and get over the school wall into the playground just as the whistle blew at 9am. Once the whistle blew, we all had to stand perfectly still and were told off if we moved. We'd then have to line up in our classes before being marched off into school.

The beginning of the day would start with assembly where we'd say the Lord's Prayer and sing a hymn. I loved 'All Things Bright and Beautiful' until some bright spark decided it should be sung to a different tune and that was then taken as being the new way of singing it. We all hated it then!

My favourite Christmas hymns included, 'Oh Little Town of Bethlehem', 'Away in a Manger', 'Once in Royal David's City', Oh Come All Ye Faithful', 'Hark the Herald Angels Sing' and 'Silent Night'. Singing hymns at Christmas certainly seemed to make you feel like Santa was on his way!

The headmaster would then give a talk on behaviour or things that were happening or going to happen. The assembly lasted for about half an hour.

Of course, for small kids, the whole thing was pretty boring so most of us just daydreamed until we had to go to our class.

There are a few assembly talks that I remember including the ones about boys misbehaving out of school (it was quite often something minor) or when boys had been spotted on school grounds after school or running along the roofs (which I did often). I remember one school assembly when the headmaster, for some unknown reason, had received a letter from Morecambe and Wise. He offered it as a prize for the best essay about autograph collecting. Although everyone thought it was great, no-one bothered entering! I wonder what happened to it? I think most kids were fed up enough with school work

A prefect's badge as worn by the older kids. Their job was to tell you to stop running in the corridor, stop talking in assembly and, if you were naughty, put your name in 'the book'. The book was then read out in assembly by the stern Deputy Headmaster. I can't remember what the punishment was but it was probably something like 'lines'.

and home work to want to write anything else in their free time.

I was quite lucky with teachers in the 1960s. They were all pretty decent although, perhaps, not so great once I was older in the 1970s.

During assembly, the deputy headmaster would get another teacher to mark where 'C' was on the piano so he could hit it before we started to sing the morning hymn. We all had to sit crossed-legged and wear coloured badges to say which 'house' we were in. These included Nelson (blue), Drake (yellow), Scott (green) and Cook (red). The Deputy Headmaster would check to see if you were wearing your badge in assembly and if you weren't, or had lost it on the way to school, you had to buy another one and write an essay about the person who your house was named after. It all seemed pretty petty to me and we were always losing our badges when we were out playing especially with rough and tumble games like British Bulldog. House points, for good work or good behaviour, were added up at the end of the week and the headmaster would hold up a board to show who had won. Once assembly was over, we'd all head off to our classes. We had a lovely female teacher, who, unlike some of the later teachers, actually seemed to like kids! Lessons were pretty basic and we also had PE which I always hated. The girls would get changed in one of the cupboards and the boys would get changed in the toilets. There was always a couple of boys who while getting changed would have a contest to see who could pee on the ceiling. The school caretaker must have dreaded going in there. PE consisted of running about, jumping star shapes, climbing ropes, balancing on bars and catching medicine balls (which weighed a ton). Our junior school PE teacher wasn't a bad bloke (unlike some of the bully-boy PE teachers in secondary schools), it was just the effort of getting changed on a freezing cold day that I didn't like. Oh, and we'd get told off if we'd forgotten our PE kit and would sometimes have to wear left over kit from the 1950s which seemed very old fashioned to us 1960s kids! We also had swimming lessons but the pool was outside, unheated, and often covered in ice! When the swimming teacher spotted that some kids looked like they were about to die of hypothermia, she would send them back indoors to get changed. One fiery teacher wasn't happy about this and sent us straight back to the swimming pool before returning to his warm, cosy staff room! In the summer, the school swimming pool would be open to 'outsiders' for a shilling a go. They were welcome to it! My birthday fell in the school summer holidays before the new term started so because of this I was soon moved up a class. All the boys liked the young female teacher and took more notice of her than they did the lessons! She reminded me at the time of one of the girls in a James Bond film.

Our lessons included reading, comprehension, writing composition, maths and painting and drawing. For good work, we'd sometimes get house points. The teacher had a draw full of gold stars which she'd stick on your work in your exercise book if it was good. Another gold star would go on a chart in the class room and, at the end of term, the person with the most stars would win a tube of Smarties. It doesn't sound much now but at the time, it was very exciting. I never won! Some kids even bought their own gold stars and stuck them on their work before they showed their parents. The teacher must have noticed but I don't remember her ever telling anyone off.

With approximately 40 children in the class, everyone knew each other although many kept to their own groups and the boys hardly ever talked to the girls. If a boy was

When it rained at break time, we would have to stay in the classroom.
There was always a big pile of comics in the corner to read. They were
mainly 'Look and Learn' but there was also the odd copy of Valiant or
Hurricane in there!

made to sit at one of the girls' tables during break on a rainy day, he'd absolutely hate it!

We'd have our milk delivered in the morning to class. At the time, there were farms nearby and the milk was delivered daily in big churns. Today, all of those farms are housing estates!

After we had our milk, it would be time for our morning playtime. Boys would run out into the playground and play football, 'it' (tag), marbles or, depending on the time of year, conkers. Every boy would have his own collection of marbles and he would challenge other boys to games to try and win more. Somehow I always lost! At the end of the year, boys would all play conkers and we'd spend evenings looking for the best horse chestnut tree. Tricks for having the longest surviving conker involved soaking them in vinegar to make them harder. They'd be put on a length of string and then smashed against an opponents conker until one smashed. While the boys were doing this, the girls would either be skipping, playing hopscotch or doing handstands against the school wall. It was unheard of for a girl to play either marbles, conkers or football. At the end of the marbles season, the person who had won most marbles would often shout 'scrambles' and throw his marbles as the other kids hurried to collect them. If it was a rainy day, we would have to stay indoors where there was a pile of comics to read including copies of the one we all found boring, 'Look and Learn'. If you were lucky, there would be a copy of the Beano or the Dandy in the pile. Once the break was over, we would all be clock watching until dinnertime.

A collection of conkers and marbles - all a boy needed to have a good time in the school playground.

Most kids stayed at school for dinner and we had to form a long queue to get into the dinner hall. Unfortunately, this took up a lot of our dinnertime. I'm not sure a lot of the time if it was worth having and included grizzly meat, long thin sausages, potatoes, carrots and gravy. My favourites were the afters which included Jam Roly Poly

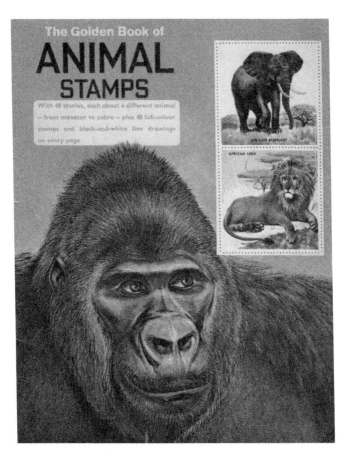

My prize for coming third in the road safety campaign at school - a book of animal stickers which you had to lick to get them to stick. I can still taste that glue!

and custard and Spotted Dick and custard. Sometimes we'd get jelly or blancmange. The dinner ladies would ask if anyone wanted seconds and hands would shoot up. I was always glad to get out of the dining hall and into the playground. Teachers were always obsessed with you eating everything on your plate and there was the threat of the cane if you didn't. I remember me and another boy left a banana in batter and made a run for it and worried all day that they'd catch up with us. Of course, they never did!

Once out in the playground, we'd play longer games such as cowboys and indians, re-enact the Second World War (we hated Germans) or play British Bulldog. A couple of kids, with their arms around each others shoulders, would start chanting, 'We won the war in 1944! We won the war in 1944!' It wasn't historically accurate but sort of rhymed so made a better chant. Very soon nearly every boy would join the line, all with their arms around each other shoulders, and any games of football had to be abandoned as war games took over. Teams were quickly drawn up and we all ran around the playground and adjoining fields machine gunning each other until one of the teachers blew the whistle.

British Bulldog was another game which took over the playground. Kids had to run from one end of the playground to the other without being caught in the middle.

Fights would occasionally break out in the playground but, as far as I remember, it was unusual if a teacher broke it up. Quite often it was just left up to the dinner ladies, some of which were battle axes that no kid would want to mess with. One of the punishments was 'to face the wall'. Sometimes the Deputy Headmaster would come along and ask you why you were there. There was always the threat of the cane although I never got it.

As we moved up a class, I found myself in Mr Smith's class. He was a very nice teacher and got on well with all of the kids. I remember once that he took the class to Paignton Zoo and an elephant pinched his umbrella. I remember the trip to the zoo with Mr Smith was 6/6 (32p).

One other thing that I remember about Mr Smith is that I was the first kid to wear blue flared jeans. Some of the kids thought this was comical and Mr Smith called them 'bell bottoms' like the ones worn by the Navy.

I can recall that Mr Smith had a reel to reel tape recorder and he would tape programmes from the radio and we would listen to them during the class. They were mainly school programmes but I think that this was all put to a stop when the BBC decided that schools shouldn't be allowed to record shows because of copyright reasons. He recorded some of the kids singing and talking on the reel to reel tapes which we all found quite funny.

In the summer, all the boys wore shorts and in the winter, they would all wear long trousers. When you went back to school after Easter and started wearing shorts again, there was always a bit of an embarrassment that you no longer had your long trousers on. Sounds daft now and pretty soon every kid in the class was wearing shorts. There was a craze for a while for the girls to wear 'Hot

Pants' but pretty quickly the teachers stamped down on this.

At the back of the classroom was a cage with gerbils in it. I can't remember if the school had any other pets. When it came to the school holidays, the kids would all put their hands up to take the gerbils home and would look after them while the school was closed. We already had a dog, two budgies and a hamster (called Scooby Doo) so I never volunteered.

In the autumn, we'd all be asked to bring in tins of food for the Harvest Festival. We'd all badger our parents for something which we'd take in the next day. A local vicar visited about once a week and everything was taken back to the church where it was later given to older people living in the area. Mr Smith was always saying that if there was an older person in your street to visit them and do chores because they might not see anyone. Many kids were in the scouts and would do bob-a-job which involved them cutting someone's grass or washing their car (if they had one).

I was never very religious but would enjoy all the bible stories especially around Easter and Christmas. At Christmas, there would be a school play and also some pupils would be chosen to sing in the choir at the local church. The Deputy Headmaster would get all the children in the hall to sing a hymn and he would go along the line listening to everyone's voice. If he tapped you on the head (which he did often!) that signified that you were in the choir. I would have rather avoided being in

69

This advert really did have every kid searching through their piggy banks to make sure that they didn't have any. Most piggy banks were full of small change like pennies and halfpennies. A half crown, the equivalent of 12½ today, went a lot further. One half crown would pay for a whole week's school dinners.

the choir but ended up in it two years running and I remember us singing 'Oh come all ye faithful' in front of everyone who had gathered in the church. I remember another year when the Deputy Head decided that our class would sing in front of the school at Christmas. As we sang, we could all hear one boy singing terrible and the Deputy Head detected this and told him to just mime! The week leading up to the Christmas holidays was great and not much work was done. On the final day, we could bring in our favourite toy, mine was always a talking tin robot that we'd brought back from Singapore.

We'd all be excited and be talking about what we wanted for Christmas which back then included things like bikes, board games (which were very popular at the time), roller skates, scooters and footballs.

After the Christmas holidays, all the boys would boast about what they got for Christmas. A lot of it was exaggerated! We'd get new exercise books for the new term and would always get the date of the year wrong for the first few weeks and would put down the previous year in our books. The first few days of the new term always seemed dull after the excitement of Christmas. It didn't seem long before we were all looking forward to our Easter break. I loved all the lead up to Easter and the many biblical stories we were read. I'm not sure how many people believed in God in the classroom (I think we were all expected to) but to us the stories were like the many other stories we read and all added to the wonder of Easter and Christmas.

There were also great exaggerations after Easter from boys saying how many chocolate eggs that they'd got. I remember being taken on several school trips , one to the local fire station and another to a nearby National Trust property. I think that we had to get our parents to sign forms and also get them to pay towards the trip.

Lessons included reading, writing, maths, geography and history. We all had to learn fractions and multiplication tables. The teacher would go around the class getting pupils to recite our tables which I hated. I remember in our last year at juniors, we had to learn binary numbers which, for a 10 year old, was confusing and boring (and ultimately pointless!). With Alan already being at the local Comprehensive, he showed me a much easier way to work out binary numbers which I showed the other kids. The teacher wasn't happy! We also had to learn long division (which I still can't do!) and long multiplication (which I eventually got the hang of).

History seemed to just consist of learning about Plymouth's 'hero', Sir Francis Drake. I remember that we built a Tudor house out of balsa wood. It seemed fantastic to me back then but probably wasn't. We also visited Drake's house at Buckland Abbey and his old haunts on the Barbican. I never remember being taught the history of any other figure from the past.

Geography just covered where Drake had been and a bit about the Maasai Warriors, whose lives we watched on the school tv and were then asked questions about. All I could remember was that they jumped about a lot!

There were several fetes and jumble sales during the year which we all loved. We were all given a bundle of admission tickets to sell (I think they were a shilling each) and we'd travel around the nearby estates, knocking on doors and trying to sell people tickets. I could never be bothered so would give them to mum to sell to her friends in the shop. The person who sold the most tickets got a prize and house points. It was never me!

Before the upcoming fete, one year, our teacher got us all to do paintings which were to be displayed in the classroom for everyone to see. Being in the infants, they probably weren't very good and I can't remember what mine was of. It was probably just a painting of our house. On the day of the fete, there were jam jars placed underneath our paintings in which people could deposit pennies for their favourite ones. Alan made sure that mine was full up and asked the teacher who had won. When he said me, Alan carried me around on his shoulders around the classroom. It was all a bit of fun and everyone was getting their friends and families to put pennies in their jars. I won a prize for the best painting when I returned to school after the holidays although I can't remember what it was. The fete also included a raffle and a jumble sale.

I remember coming away with bundles of comics and annuals as well as various toys including a tin typewriter and a Magic Robot game.

Outside, there would be pony rides and I remember going on them a couple of times. It was hard to walk afterwards! There were lots of games where you could win things and Alan and me would be back and forwards to the fete occasionally returning home with our 'spoils'. One particular fete that I remember was when our PE teacher was running a stall in the canteen and a boy, who had left the school a couple of years earlier, came back and punched him right in the nose nearly knocking him out. Everyone liked the teacher so it seemed quite upsetting at the time. If he'd punched one of the other

teachers, perhaps I wouldn't have been so bothered!
Mr Smith had one of those contraptions set up where you
had to take a metal hoop around a twisted metal wire
without it touching and making a buzzing noise. Mr
Smith was always very inventive and his classes were a
lot of fun. He had a glass eye which some pupils can
remember him taking out but I never remember him
doing that.

I didn't particularly like school and spent a lot of my time
daydreaming but I can see now, recalling the school fetes,
that some teachers put in a lot of effort to make the kids
happy. The strict Deputy Headmaster even had a stall
where he'd made a board with corks with numbers on the
bottom. If you picked certain numbers, you won a prize.
You sort of saw a different side to some teachers at the
fetes than you did in the classroom. They were happier -
almost human!

We had a road safety poster drawing competition one
year and I painted a picture of a big zebra crossing
(which is what all the other kids were painting!). I came
third and was awarded a book of animal stickers which
I've still got. The results even made it into the local
paper! I don't know how the judges chose between all the
various paintings of zebra crossings which all looked
much the same!

School in the 1960s was a lot of fun, when I think back to
it, although it still seemed like prison to me and I would
run all the way home as soon as they let us out at 4pm!

Classrooms always had plenty of Look and Learn comics for you to read when it rained during break times. Parents and teachers probably thought that they were very educational but we would have preferred the Beano or the Dandy!

Money boxes came in all shapes and sizes and the most popular were piggy banks, safes or post boxes. This one shows a police telephone box which was made more popular because of tv's Doctor Who.

Three

Toys and Games

The 1960s seemed to have some of the best toys
including Lego, Meccano, Scalextric, Matchbox and
Dinky cars and wonderful board games. At the beginning
of the 1960s, games seemed more basic with well
established games, including card games, being played by
the whole family. As the decade moved on, the toys
seemed to get better and better. Perhaps manufacturers
and advertisement people realised that there was a huge
market producing and selling children's toy. At the
beginning of the 1960s, every boy wanted a train set but
by the end of the 1960s, through advertising, there were
many must-have toys such as Lego, Spacehoppers,
Action Man, Mouse Trap, Subbuteo, Etch A Sketch,
Rock 'Em Sock 'Em Robots, Hotwheels Racers, soldiers,
cowboys, anything to do with Thunderbirds and many
more.

Me playing with my Lego on a hot sunny day in about 1966. The things you could build were endless although I always built an aeroplane or a train! The old spice and cigarettes were for my dad's birthday.

For older boys, there were model kits to make which included aircraft, cars, spaceships, astronauts and historical figures. The most popular kits of the time were made by Airfix but their rivals, Revell and Frog were also extremely popular.

In the later 1960s, anything to do with space travel was very sought after. Every boy wanted an Airfix Saturn V rocket, Lunar Orbiter or Lunar Module. We all had them hanging from our bedroom ceilings.

Me on my 5th birthday with my favourite toy - a talking tin robot. It said 6 phrases of which my favourite was, 'I am bulletproof too - ha, ha, ha!' which I would copy whenever I could get anyone to listen!

Corgi cars were very popular with boys. When Goldfinger was released in 1965, every boy wanted the Corgi Aston Martin DB5 featured in the film. They came complete with ejector seat, machine guns and bulletproof shield. Many of the little men that came with it which were fired from the ejector seat, soon became lost. The packaging was very colourful and worth keeping but, at the time, was the first thing to go straight in the bin! What boy wanted to keep the packaging when he had James Bond's car to drive around his bedroom or the garden?

Most of the cars came in gold although the one in the film was actually silver.

There were many other Corgi television and film tie-in cars. One of the most remembered was the Batmobile which featured Batman and Robin.

Every boy had their own Corgi Batmobile and re-enacted scenes that they'd seen on the popular tv programme starring Adam West and Burt Ward. Mine was regularly driven around our bedroom, the front room and shot off ramps in the back garden. I'm amazed that it survived!

It fired rockets (soon lost), had a spring-loaded chain cutter that appeared from the front of the car and moving flames from the rear thruster.

Together with the James Bond car, it is one of the best-remembered (and often kept) Corgi vehicles of the 1960s.

When The Man From Uncle hit the screens in 1964, every boy wanted their own Oldsmobile Thrushbuster although it wasn't until 1966 that Corgi first released their own version of the vehicle. It featured gun-firing characters which were operated by pushing the periscope on top of the car. It came complete with a Waverley Ring showing photos of the show's two main characters, Napoleon Solo and Illya Kuryakin. The show spawned an array of merchandise and toys including bubblegum cards, toy guns, badges, walkie talkies, dolls, games and much more.

I remember us pestering our mum and dad for extra pocket money so that we could buy this car. The Man From Uncle was the coolest thing on tv in the 1960s!

The Corgi Man From Uncle 'Thrushbuster' which came complete with a Waverley ring featuring one of the characters from the show.

The Avengers was also very popular in the 1960s and Corgi released cars featuring Steed's red Bentley and Emma Peel's white Lotus. These were never quite as popular as James Bond's DB5, the Batmobile or the Thrushbuster and seem to have been much forgotten over the years.

We all loved *Daktari* and Clarence the cross-eyed lion. Corgi released a camouflaged Land Rover complete with animals and other vehicles. It mustn't have sold as well as other vehicles because years later, the Landrover was given away free in a Tarzan related cereal promotion.

Any toy to do with Thunderbirds, rockets or space travel was
sure to be a hit with boys.

Overseas, the Green Hornet's Black Beauty was just as popular as the Thrushbuster but not as popular in the UK because the show had been banned from our screens supposedly due to the violence which was no worse than that found in *Batman* or *The Man from Uncle*.

Dinky cars were more expensive but were still much sought after. They featured well-known cars and lorries but their most popular vehicles were probably the one that related to Gerry Anderson's many television shows. These included Joe 90's futuristic car, Captain Scarlet's Spectrum Control car, the Captain Scarlet Maximum Security vehicle, Lady Penelope's pink Rolls Royce, Sam's car from Joe 90 and later Ed Straker's car and the Interceptor from *UFO*.

By far the most popular toys were the ones relating to Thunderbirds particularly the much-desired Thunderbird 2 which every boy wanted.

Dinky vehicles also produced many military vehicles which included tanks, planes and jeeps etc.

The most affordable and well-loved toy cars came from Matchbox which featured a range of modern cars as well as lorries, vans, police cars, ambulances, tractors, ice cream vans etc all in their own individual boxes. Most shops had a display of Matchbox cars and every boy had a collection which he'd roll down banks or tracks or push around the front room.

Board games were very well liked in the 1960s and the most popular of these was Monopoly. Every family seemed to have a set and a game of Monopoly could go on for hours.

Boys loved Airfix kits and many would have model planes hanging from their ceilings. Other kits included spacecraft, ships, submarines and cars.

Mouse Trap was also a lot of fun and sections were added as players threw dice and travelled around the board. It was very inventive and kept us all quiet for hours.

There were so many new games released in the 1960s that it's hard to list them all but ones that we enjoyed playing included Cluedo (a whodunnit game), Beetle, Battleships, Formula 1, Tip-it, Ker Plunk, Shenanigans (a fairground board game), Spy ring and Blast-Off!

Tv related board games included Z Cars, Captain Scarlet, Thunderbirds, The Man From Uncle, Dr Kildare and Doctor Who.

There were other games that had been around for years including Scrabble, Tiddlywinks, Snakes and Ladders, Ludo, Blow Football, Dominoes, Chess and Checkers.

Card games included Happy Families and Snap.

Other games included Escalado, Penalty and Scoop.

Anything to do with robots was very popular and one of the best-selling games of the time was Magic Robot. It looked far more interesting on tv than it was in real life (like many games!).

Action Man was a favourite with boys and we'd dangle him out of the window on rope, drop him from great heights on home-made parachutes (usually a hanky and some string!), have mock battles and drive him in tanks and jeeps down hills and around the garden.

Every boy had a collection of Timpo cowboys and Indians together with forts, wigwams and ranches. Airfix soldiers were also popular and we'd have mock battles on the dining room table. The Japanese and Germans always came out the worst.

Spacehoppers came out in the late 1960s and early 1970s. We all wanted one and most of us got one for our birthdays or at Christmas. I used to bounce mine up and down the front room and out in the garden!

For one Christmas, we got a table football set with handles so you could flick the players and spin them around to kick the ball into goal. We loved it and would play for hours. Until then, they were the sort of things you only saw at Butlin's or in amusement arcades. Rocket Racers and Hotwheel tracks were also popular. Rocket tracks were red and Hotwheel ones were orange. We'd have them set up so cars did loop-de-loop or jumped across gaps. Sometimes we'd set the track up so it left the house and went out into the garden. The cars certainly took a lot of knocking about. Scalextric sets let you race the cars round and round a track. The advert on the telly always showed them going on for miles but most tracks just went around in a big circle or a figure of eight. The most desired toy of 1969 must have been the Spacehopper. All kids had them and we'd all be up at the local garage pumping them up with their free air. That was before health and safety rules came in and they decided that it wasn't safe to let kids anywhere near garage air pumps. Pumping up a Spacehopper with a bike pump seemed to take forever and then, when you'd finished, you were too worn out to go on it!

There were certainly some excellent toys in the 1960s and we all had our favourites. Mine will always be the classic toys like Monopoly, Mouse Trap, Corgi and Dinky cars, Meccano, my Space Hopper and the amazing football table!

If you were an avid model maker, you would often paint your finished
car, boat or plane with Humbrol paints. This took a lot of patience,
which most kids didn't have., because the paint took a while to dry.
Most boys got much of the paint on themselves and their clothes so
many models went unpainted!

Four

Outdoor activities

Every kid played outside in the 1960s. Living near to woods, we were always looking for materials to build our new dens which, back then, seemed quite elaborate at times! Living in a newish house meant that the rest of the street was still being built so, as soon as the workmen had knocked off for the day, we'd be straight along to the building site to look for new materials for our dens.
The excitement of the half built houses and walls meant that it could be quite a while before we left the site. We'd run along the walls and jump off at height pretending to be Batman, Superman or Joe 90. We'd set up cans and bottles on the lower walls and shoot them off with catapults, potato guns or even home made bows and arrows. Half built houses with no staircases led to us climbing up planks to get to the top floor. We had no sense of danger, perfect balance and it was very rare for anyone to come to any harm.

Summer holidays were filled with building dens, building go-karts, riding bikes and generally exploring. The woods and its creeks and ponds made a good place to look for old bike wheels for go-karts, we regularly got stuck in the mud up to our waists! On other days, we would search for frogs and tadpoles. Every boy had a jam jar full of tadpoles on his kitchen window. The thrill of stalking wildlife came from tv shows and I-Spy books and we'd regularly go out looking for badgers, foxes, bats, squirrels and mice. We hardly ever saw anything so were amazed when a family of foxes moved into the bank across from our house. Every morning, a young fox would peek out of its den, showing no fear, and just watch us go by. It wasn't long before every kid in the area knew where it was and it scarpered soon after.

The park was always full of kids riding on the see-saw, slides. swings and roundabouts. Some parks had more exotic rides such as witches hats and hobby horses. The local park was probably the place where there was most injuries. The ground was made of hard concrete and many kids managed to injure themselves by running around too fast of coming off the swings and slide at speed.

The nearby hill was great for riding bikes down or just running as fast as you could. Sometimes you would run so fast that you couldn't stop and would almost clear the adjoining football field.

If there were kids in the park that you knew, it was a good opportunity to get together and have a game of cowboys and Indians or a 'game of war'. We'd either be running around whooping like Red Indians or pretending to machine gun Germans!

A collection of I-Spy books which could be bought for a shilling and featured a range of subjects including cars, insects, trees, butterflies and birds etc. The books were run in conjunction with the article in the News Chronicle (later the Daily Mail) which was headed by the Red Indian, Chief I-Spy.

Kids, when playing war games, would ask another kid if he wanted to be shot by machine gun or bow and arrow. If it was machine gun, the first kid would make his arms into a maching gun shape and make a tat-a-tat-tat noise as the other kid would roll about on the floor. It was similar with a bow and arrow except the other kid would clutch his chest before collapsing. We all really just copied what we'd seen on tv and in the cinema.

All the kids had dens but were reluctant to tell the other kids where they were in case they wrecked them. This happened often and you could find your wonderfully camouflaged den, pulled apart and destroyed.

In the winter, when it snowed, we'd return to the building site and climb the mound of mud there and pretend to be arctic explorers. We'd call it Mount Everest! We'd look for mysterious creature's footprints and if there weren't any, we'd make our own including those of exotic animals such as Gorillas and Yetis! We probably got the idea from watching Scooby Doo!

Playing football (the posher kids played cricket!), having bike races, having secret clubs, building dens or just generally getting up to mischief all seemed part of a summer holiday. Looking back, it's hard to remember a day when we weren't out and about or a day when the sun wasn't shining. I suppose it must have rained sometimes during our school holidays but my memory, perhaps, has just remembered the best of times having endless fun in the long hot days of summer.

Five

Childhood illnesses

I think I had every childhood illness going during my first seven years including measles, German measles and mumps. We were all told that once we'd had them, we'd never get them again. It wasn't true, I got German measles twice!

Being sick, getting coughs and sneezes and headaches all seemed worse when you were a kid. Mum would rub Vick on my chest when I had a very bad cough, as did most mothers. Your chest seemed to get a lot sorer when you were a kid coughing. I've never had coughs like that since.

Some kids at school had more 'exotic' illnesses like tonsillitis, glandular fever and appendicitis. Boys who had had their tonsils out would boast when they got back to school that they'd been given endless supplies of ice cream in hospital to soothe their sore throat. It almost made it all sound worthwhile. Kids who had their appendix removed always wanted to show you the scar. Our teacher said that we didn't need it and it was only there from the days when we used to eat grass. He would come out with lots of stories like that and it was only later that I realised that most of them were nonsense.

A trip to the doctor involved waiting in a converted house with copies of Woman's Realm and National Geographic in the waiting room. Everyone who went to the doctor got the same treatment. He'd listen to your chest with a stethoscope and look at your throat and make you say, 'arrrgghhh'. It didn't matter what you went in for, the treatment was always the same. You usually ended up with a bottle of pink penicillin which I quite liked the taste of! I don't remember anyone having blood tests (that seems to be a recent thing) or all the other tests you have today.

The school doctor was another proposition. School checks always seemed to result in them getting you to drop your trousers. Occasionally, they would ask you to cough. I'm still not entirely sure what it was all about! We'd also have a nit nurse who would check us all with fine combs for head lice. She was pretty grim and I don't remember her ever finding any. There was also the hearing specialist who would whisper behind your head and the eye specialist who would show you an array of coloured dots and ask if you could see the numbers within them. We all felt like we'd passed an exam when we got it right.

I convinced myself that the school dentist was actually a war criminal on the run. He was the right age but didn't have a German accent. He delighted in drilling teeth and never used any sort of anaesthetic. I think he put me off dentists for life. Occasionally, we'd be given gas when he wanted to rip some of our teeth out and I can still remember the smell of the rubber mask he put over my face! It wasn't until later that I realised some kids had their own dentist - I thought that you had to see the school dentist! They talked of things I'd never heard of like numbing injections and Novocaine. In my head, I had a plan when I grew up to go back and visit the school dentist, strap him to the chair and drill all of his teeth. Fortunately, he emigrated! It was only a daydream though, something I did often at school.

The only other 'illness' that inflicted kids at school were verrucas. Normally, they appeared on the sole of your foot but Alan had one on his hand which meant a trip to the doctor. Nowadays, the treatment is to either leave it alone or use one of the over-the-counter painless remedies. In the 1960s, the solution was too burn it out. Alan wasn't too happy but mum bought him a fantastic Marvel annual for going (which I enjoyed reading also without going through any of the pain).

The only good thing about being ill is that you would get some time off school. Often the doctor would come around and visit you if you were particularly poorly. The examination was the same - the stethoscope and a look down your throat.

I'm sure there were many more childhood illnesses about that luckily I avoided and having a day, or even a week off school, always compensated for it!

The playground held many dangers for kids from the metal climbing frames, concrete floors, steam engines containing asbestos, roundabouts, witches hats, swings, roundabouts and see-saws. We would sometimes come home with cuts and bruises but we had great fun at the same time!

Six

Sweets and Chocolate

A trip to the local sweet shop was always something to look forward to. Many sweets were stored in large jars and most kids' pocket money would be spent on their favourites. These included Fruit Salads and Black Jacks (8 for a penny), flying saucers, chocolate mice, bon bons and chewy bananas. Mum worked at the local shop so we would always pop in after school to see what we could get. Sweets and chocolates seemed more of a treat back then.

My favourites were Caramac (it doesn't taste the same today!), Maltesers and Animal Bars. You could collect the different wrappers of Animal Bars and stick them in an album. We all liked collecting things then so this was great. I loved Milky Bars too (don't most kids?). There were always competition on the wrappers to win things like cowboy outfits. Collecting the wrappers meant that you could send off for things like free cowboys and

A badge given away free with Nestles Milky Bar.

Indians or water pistols. Everything seemed to come with a free gift in the 1960s.

There was always bubblegum cards which kids had to have. I can still remember the smell of the bubblegum that came with football cards and cards from popular tv shows such as The Champions and Captain Scarlet. None of us were ever much interested in the bubble gum and we'd all be in the playground the next day with our 'swaps'. The manufacturers obviously printed far more copies of particular cards so you ended up with the same ones and had to keep buying more.

Cadbury's Fruit and Nut had it's own advert and their products also came with free stuff such as badges. We all had huge collections of badges which were also given away with ice cream, lollies and other products.

A trip to the sweet shop also gave you a chance to delve into the big freezer that stocked all the Lyons Maid and Walls ice lollies such as Fab and Zoom. I was never quite big enough to reach to the bottom.

To jog your memory, some of the most popular sweets and chocolates of the day included chocolate bars such as Mackintosh's Toffee Crisp, Marathon, Fry's Medley, Cadbury's Brazil Nut, Fry's Chocolate Cream (at 7d), Cadbury's Dairy Milk, Coffee Crisp, Cadbury's Strawberry (6d), Cracknel, Cadbury's Skippy, Flake, Nestles Milky Bar, Milk Chocolate Aero, Nux, Galaxy, Cadbury's Nut Crisp, Nestles Brazil Nut, Cadbury's Fruit and Nut, Kit Kat, Cadbury's Lucky Numbers, Cadbury's Super Moose, Fry's Chocolate Delight, Animal Bars, Cadbury's Bar Six, Cadbury's Golden Crisp, Twix,

A badge given away with Cadbury's Fruit and Nut.

George Best was one of the most popular football players in the 1960s and there were many bubblegum cards featuring his images which were much sought after by boys.

Duncan Gingernut Chocolate, Cadbury's Peppermint,
Cadbury's Strawberry, Mackintosh's Caramac Minty
Fudge (at 6d), Cadbury's Extra, Fry's Bliss, Fry's Tiffin
with biscuits and nuts (6d), Mackintosh's Loot,
Mackintosh's Golden Cup (6d), 5 Boys (8d), Parisian
Creams, Cadbury's Roasted Almond (9d) and Cadbury's
Golden Crisp (at one shilling).
Other sweets included Toffo, Smarties in tubes as well as
boxes, Rowntree's Jelly Tots, Galaxy Counters (at 6d),
All Chocolate Treets, Rowntree's Fruit Pastilles,
Mackintosh's Tooty Frooties, Polos, Munchies,
Lovehearts, Life Savers, Spangles, Payne's Chocolate
Peanuts (at 6d), Cadbury's Summer Fruits, Iced
Caramels, Paynes Assorted Poppets, Opal Fruits,
Buttersnap (at 6d), Topic, Cadbury's Twenties, Maltesers
For mums and dads, there were After Eights, Dairy Box,
Milk Tray and Mint Chocs.
Some wrappers contained pictures that you could save
and stick in albums. A lot of the fun was the actual
packaging (although most of us loved what was inside). I
wish that I'd kept some of it now!
I probably tried every sweet and chocolate bar during the
1960s but most are long forgotten.

Seven

Fashions

It's hard to believe now but, in the late 1960s, there were some kids who turned up at school not just wearing bell-bottoms (as our teacher called them) but also cravats. Flowery shirts were also in for a while at school for the boys. It seems odd now because the school had a uniform that everyone was meant to wear but, looking back at old school photos, it doesn't seem like many of us took much notice. Fashionable girls turned up at junior school in hot pants which, for a while neither the parents or pupils minded but then there was an objection from one of the teachers and they were soon banned. It's funny how the fashions of the day filtered down into the playground. Most of the time, I turned up in my home-knitted maroon jumper, white shirt and school trousers or shorts (if it was summer). Things must have changed though because I was soon wearing my flared trousers and favourite jumper to school. Outside school, fashions included mini skirts and maxi skirts, hot pants (for girls, of course), corduroys, snazzy shirts and winkle picker shoes. Most of it passed me by although I did get mum to make me a Jason King cravat which I wore for a whole day!

Clothes at the beginning of the 1960s were more dull but became more trendy and colourful as the decade moved on.

Ladybird produced many fashionable clothes for kids which were small-scale versions of what their parents wore. Girls particularly liked being fashionable, especially at school, and the school uniform seemed to disappear almost completely by the late 1960s although it was still apparently compulsory.

This is about as trendy as I got in the 1960s. Bell-bottom jeans and a jumper with a sewn in polo-neck. I wore these to school also!

Fashions varied greatly during the 1960s although most didn't seem to filter down to us. There were many fashions running side by side as worn by Rockers, Mods and Hippies. For adults, the hippy influence produced tie-dye and batik fabrics, bell-bottoms and paisley prints. Mary Quant introduced the mini skirt in 1964 and with it went matching hairstyles and huge false eyelashes. Our mums all had a pair!

Carnaby Street and Chelsea's King's Road were seen as the place to see the current fashions and many people were influenced by the models of the day including Twiggy, Jean Shrimpton, Colleen Corby, Penelope Tree and Veruschka. Photographers like Cecil Beaton, David Bailey and Richard Avedon produced iconic images that highlighted the fashions of the day.

As a young boy, I suppose we were all influenced by fashion but not so much as some of the crazy styles in popular magazines.

To get a proper feel of the fashions of the day, and many were crazy, just watch an old episode of Department S (particularly Jason King) or one of the many other hip and trendy shows of the day such as The Avengers or The Prisoner.

106

Eight

Radio

Radio played a big part in many families lives as most didn't own a television set. We probably had a radio long before we had a television set and I remember my parents listening to it often.

In the early 1960s, in the days before Radio 1 and Radio 2, the BBC broadcasted the Light Programme. The service began in 1945 and continued until 1967 when it was renamed Radio 2.

One of the most popular programmes listened to on the radio at the time was The Archers. The show commenced in 1950 and attracted huge audiences.

Housewives' Choice ran from 1946 to 1967 and was broadcast every morning. It was a request show designed to entertain housewives during the day.

The Light Programme ceased on 30th September 1967 on the same day that Radio 1 commenced.

The Disc Jockeys on Radio 1 were mainly culled from

A copy of Radio Times from the late 1960s featuring Simon Dee on the cover.

pirate stations such as Radio Caroline. Caroline had broadcast out at sea, just outside British territorial waters, to avoid broadcasting laws. They first started

A popular 'Dansette' radio from the 1960s.

broadcasting on 27th March 1964. In April 1964, Radio Atlanta followed suit broadcasting from a former coaster, the MV Mi Amigo. Tony Benn, the British Postmaster General, introduced a bill to parliament which effectively outlawed pirate radio stations.

Many of the 1960s best remembered DJs began their careers on pirate radio including Tony Blackburn, Emperor Rosko, John Peel, Johnnie Walker and Kenny

Everett. When Radio 1 set up in 1967, it employed many of the most popular stars of pirate radio.

Trying to record the charts on my dad's reel-to-reel tape recorder was something we did on most Sundays. Everyone had to be quiet because the microphone had to be placed beside the radio and picked up every sound. Occasionally, one of us would forget that it was recording and we'd accidentally sing along to the track. Once it was all on tape, we'd listen to our favourite tracks over and over again. Some of my favourites were *Sugar Sugar* by *The Archies* and *In the Year 2525* by *Zager and Evans*.

Radio Luxembourg had been a favourite for years. Broadcasting from Luxembourg to Ireland and Britain, the service began in 1933. We all loved tuning in at night when the reception was better although still far from perfect. Many shows were recorded in London and broadcast from Luxembourg to avoid broadcasting legislation laws. There were lots of competitions and featured many of our favourite DJs including Barry Alldis, Chris Denning, Colin Hamilton, Ted King, Johnny Moran, Don Moss and Don Wardell. Many London-based DJs recorded their shows at Radio Luxembourg's studios at 38 Hertford Street in London. These included Peter Aldersley, Sam Costa, Alan Dell, Keith Fordyce, Alan Freeman, David Gell, Tony Hall, Jack Jackson, David Jacobs, Brian Matthew, Don Moss, Pete Murray, Ray Orchard, Jimmy Savile, Shaw Taylor, Jimmy Young and Muriel Young.

A typical week of Luxembourg consisted of:

Sundays: 6:00 pm - Butlin's Beaver Club – *with Uncle Eric Winstone*.
8:30 pm - Take Your Pick with Michael Miles.
9:30 pm – This I Believe. The Edward R Murrow show presented by Sir Basil Bartlett.
Mondays: 9:30 pm – Candid Microphone – *starring listeners caught in the act*.
11:15 pm – Frank and Ernest - *religion from the Dawn Bible Students Association.*
11:30 pm – The World Tomorrow with Herbert W Armstrong *later heard on Tuesdays as well replacing* Oral Roberts.
Tuesdays: 9:00 pm – Lucky Number – *with Keith Fordyce*.
10:00 pm – The Capitol Show – *Mel Thompson presenting Capitol Records new releases.*
Wednesdays: 8:00 pm – Double Your Money with Hughie Green.
10:00 pm – Rockin' To Dreamland – *with Keith Fordyce playing the latest British and American hit records.*
11:30 pm – The Hour of Decision with Billy Graham.
Thursdays: 8:30 pm – Lucky Couple – *with David Jacobs recorded on location in the UK.*
9:30 pm – Irish Requests.
10:45 pm – Italy Sings – *presented by the Italian State Tourist Office*.
Fridays: 10:30 pm – Record Hop – *Benny Lee presents the latest Columbia and Parlophone Records.*

Saturdays: 7:00 pm – Amateur Football – *results of the matches played today*.

8:00 pm – Jamboree – *120 minutes of exciting, non-stop, action-packed radio ..."Teenage Jury" and at approximately 9:30: Alan Freed the remarkable American disc-jockey whose programmes in the States cause excitement to rise to a fever pitch, presents "Rock 'n' roll"*.

10.00 PM – Tonight – Peter Haigh *presents news, music and personalities recorded at the Embassy Club in London*.

10:30 pm – Philips' Fanfare – *records from this label presented by Guy Standeven*.

Radio Luxembourg is remembered for playing all our favourite hits and the songs that the BBC wouldn't play but there was also a lot of religion thrown in! Popular quiz shows like Hughie Green's *Double Your Money* and Michael Miles' *Take Your Pick* took off on Luxembourg before becoming big hits on television.

Radio in the 1960s seemed the best and with Luxembourg, the pirate stations and the introduction of Radio 1, we could always hear all our favourite tunes.

Nine

Television

Most families in the 1960s rented their televisions from outlets such as DER for a cost of 25 - 30 shillings a month. Early models were table-top appliances with 12 - 17 inch screens. All had wooden surrounds and the more modern models came with their own thin 1960's-type legs.

Once you'd chosen the model that you wanted, it would be delivered to your home and a technician would set it up. To many people, television was a relatively new thing which had only really taken off with the Coronation of Queen Elizabeth II. Televisions had appealing model names such as Starmaster, the Consolette and the Major. When I think back to the 1960s, I remember watching all those wonderful programmes that were on at the time in full colour. It's funny how your memory plays tricks with you because we all had black and white sets. There were no remote controls and the tv had to be tuned in with a

We all loved Doctor Who and would have loved to have won a full size Dalek in one of the many competitions that featured in comics and magazines at the time. This photo shows my own Dalek which I built years later - it eventually ended up on ebay!

dial. My parents were always saying, 'Derek - turn the telly over!'. By the early 1960s, there were only two channels - BBC 1 and ITV. ITV was made up of many regional stations.

When I was very little, my favourite programmes were Andy Pandy, Bill and Ben and Gerry Anderson's Fireball XL5. There's no doubt that the 1960s had some of the best television programmes and some of my favourites included Lost in Space, Star Trek, Department S, Randall Hopkirk, The Avengers, Captain Scarlet and the

114

Mysterons, The Champions, Danger Man, Doctor Who, Joe 90, The Saint, Stingray and Thunderbirds. There were many other excellent shows. Watching The Flaxton Boys followed by The Golden Shot always reminded me there was school the next day and, in some ways, ruined the weekend.

There's programmes on the telly in the 1960s that we never missed including I Dream of Jeannie, Bewitched, Opportunity Knocks, Crossroads, Coronation Street and Z-Cars (I loved Z-Cars).

Of course, being a small boy, I loved all the cartoons on at the time including The Flintstones (adults watched it too at the time), Casper the Ghost, Secret Squirrel, Yogi Bear, Superman and Top Cat (renamed Boss Cat in the UK because there was a cat food available called Top Cat) and Atom Ant. There were many, many more including the regulars such as Bugs Bunny, Daffy Duck and the Road Runner. Later in the 1960s, there were classic cartoons that we all loved like Wacky Races with Dick Dastardly and Muttley as well as Scooby-Doo, Where are You?

I'd get back from school and if mum wasn't home yet from the shop, I'd lie on the couch, put my duffle coat over my head, with just a small bit to peep out, and watch the telly. I never ventured upstairs because, being only 7, I suppose I imagined there might be ghosts or something. The programme that was always first on was Paulus the Wood Gnome which, with his jerky movements, was enough to give anyone the creeps! It was some strange Scandinavian puppet show, which I didn't like, but it was

115

One of my favourite annuals from the 1960s featuring The Flintstones.
We all loved the show even our parents!

the only thing on. This was followed by the Australian cartoon, 'King Arthur and his Square Knights of the Round Table'. Once mum and Alan were home, I was quite happy and forgot all about the creepiness of the house when I first got in!

In between all the programmes on ITV, a local announcer would come on to tell you about the next programme and upcoming programmes during the day. In the Westward region, where I lived, there was also Gus Honeybun's birthdays and there was much excitement if your name was read out on the 5 minute slot and Gus, who was a

A badge from Westward Tv's Gus Honeybun Show.

rabbit puppet, would perform tricks. Sometimes, you could clearly see the arm of his operator but we all loved it. If your birthday was read out, all the kids would be talking about it at school the next day.

By far my favourite show towards the end of the 1960s was Randall and Hopkirk (Deceased) starring Kenneth Cope and Mike Pratt. All the kids at school loved it and they would always say the next day, 'Did you see Randall

EIGHTPENCE

Radio Times

INTRODUCING

The Swinging New
Radio Service

BBC TV Plans
for the Autumn

The Radio Times
Weekly
Magazine Feature
STAR STORIES
IN COLOUR
this week
SAMMY DAVIS Jnr.
COOKERY
GARDENING
MOTORING

A Radio Times magazine feature a cover promoting the BBC's new
radio station, Radio 1 described as 'the swinging new radio service'.

118

and Hopkins last night?'. Hopkirk always got called Hopkins at our school (and probably everywhere else) because Mary Hopkin was very popular at the time. Another programme I absolutely loved was 'Land of the Giants' which used to be on soon after I came home from school. All the kids loved it and we collected bubblegum cards and swapped them in the street. I remember one dinnertime at school when one of the boys said that he'd seen 'little people' running amongst the grass. It sounds crazy now but soon every kid was saying they could see them. It ended with a dinner lady saying, 'Don't be so silly!' and then the whistle was blown for the end of the break and it was all soon forgotten. It's hard to imagine today, the effect that television had on kids in the 1960s. Nowadays, we all know how every scene is filmed, about special effects, stuntmen etc but back then, to us, it all seemed very real.

BBC's Doctor Who gave all children nightmares. William Hartnell was the first Doctor but I really got into the show when Patrick Troughton took over the role. Alan and me would act out all the parts as we played outside which included being Daleks, Cybermen and Yetis. Watching the 1960s show nowadays, it perhaps doesn't look as slick as the modern version but watching the programme on a black and white set somehow made the show seem a lot creepier. I'm sure most kids thought the Daleks and Cyberman were real. We did a competition to win a Dalek but didn't win which was just as well because it wouldn't have fitted in well at our naval flat at Devonport and we would have both probably been scared of it!

119

All kids loved the Lone Ranger cartoon which first aired in 1966. To tie in with the series, Lone Ranger Wafers were brought out.

Tv stations always shut down every night and a local presenter would wish you a good night and remind you to unplug your telly. Everyone was scared to leave their telly plugged in overnight in case it suddenly caught alight but I never heard of it happening to anyone. 'God Save the Queen' would play and then the presenter, a few minutes later, would again remind you to unplug the telly before a loud whistling noise was heard and the signal was switched off.

 A typical BBC Saturday viewing in 1968 included:

10.00 am Developing a Small Firm.

10.30 am Suivez La Piste.

(which only went on to 11.00 am and then there was a gap in transmission).

120

12.00 pm The Weather Man.

12.05 pm Laurel and Hardy.

12.25 pm ZOKKO!

12.45 pm Grandstand
which included:
12.55 pm Fight of the Week
1.20 pm Football Preview
1.30 pm Professional Tennis
1.50 pm Racing
2.05 pm Amateur Boxing
2.20 pm Racing
2.35 pm Amateur Boxing
2.50 pm Racing
3.10 pm Rugby League
3.25 pm Ice Hockey
3.45 pm Rugby League
4.25 pm Ice Hockey
4.40 pm Teleprinter
4.46 pm Ice Hockey
4.55 Results Service

5.15 pm Dr Who

5.40 pm The News

5.50 Tom and Jerry

FOR STORIES AND PICTURES—SEE PAGE 4

For a while, The Monkees were just as big as The Beatles and appeared on magazines and newspapers everywhere. Their tv show was incredibly popular and most kids wouldn't miss it.

Ten

The Cinema

We loved going to the cinema and especially loved
Disney films. Mum and dad would take us often. One of
the first films that I remember seeing was Disney's 'Mary
Poppins' in 1964 which starred Julie Andrews and Dick
Van Dyke.

Although I was just 4 at the time, we also saw the James
Bond film 'Goldfinger'. Being very small, I think I fell
asleep before the end! James Bond was very popular with
boys and we all had to have a Corgi 007 Aston Martin
complete with ejector seat.

Batman (1966) was another incredibly popular film with
kids because of the tv series starring Adam West and
Burt Ward. When we weren't pretending to be Tarzan or
James Bond, we were happily jumping off the school
roof pretending to be Batman.

Alan took me to see 'Born Free' in 1966 and mum met us
at the cinema. She said that I was crying because the lion
had died! Whenever I hear Matt Monroe singing 'Born

An ABC Film Review magazine from December 1966 showing Raquel Welch and John Richardson in 'One Million Years BC'.

Free', it always takes me back to 1966 although I don't think I've seen the film since. There was a very popular tv series later on called 'Living Free' in 1972.

I also loved Winnie the Pooh and the Honey Tree which came out in 1966.

The following year, 1967, had two fantastic films, 'Doctor Doolittle' starring Rex Harrison and Disney's 'Jungle Book'.

Both films were incredibly popular with kids and even back then, there was much merchandise. I remember having a jigsaw of Doctor Doolittle caring for a horse wearing spectacles! The characters of Jungle Book were everywhere including on breakfast cereal and chocolate. Kids liked to make things then and there would be cardboard cut-outs of the back of cereal boxes to make your favourite characters from the film. Baloo was the most popular. The songs from the film became very popular especially 'The Bare Necessities' and 'I Wanna Be Like You'.

We saw lots of films in 1969 but the ones I remember best are Blackbeard's Ghost starring Peter Ustinov, Winnie the Pooh and the Blustery Day and the blockbuster of the year, Chitty Chitty Bang Bang, again starring Dick Van Dyke.

In the late 1960s, Alan and me would sometimes go to the Saturday morning cinema club in town. There were cartoons, shorter serial-type dramas (I never did see the end of any of them) and a main film. All members of the cinema club got a badge. I loved the serials but Alan wouldn't always take me so they were hard to follow. I

A Saturday morning cinema children's club badge.

remember one film we saw was Tarzan and the Trappers starring Gordon Scott. It had been made 10 years earlier but Tarzan was very popular because of the tv show which every boy loved. We'd all try and copy the famous Tarzan call (with little success) as we played in the nearby woods.

When gran came down in the summer, she would take us to the pictures also. I remember seeing 'The Love Bug' which featured Herbie, the Volkswagen with its own mind, in 1968. She also took us to 'The Computer wore Tennis Shoes' which starred Kurt Russell and came out in 1969.

Mum and dad took us to see the latest James Bond film, 'On Her Majesty's Secret Service' in 1969 at the nearby State cinema. At the time, there were smaller cinemas everywhere and this one was handy for us as it wasn't far away. I'd seen nearly all of the James Bond films even though I was only 8 years old. Even so, I didn't notice that James Bond was played by a different actor (George Lazenby) in the same way that every time I saw a Tarzan film, he was played by someone else. In those days, there were cartoons (even if it was an adult show), lots of adverts (trying to sell you allsorts including hot dogs and ice lollies) and two feature films. It would always take a while for the major films to reach the smaller cinemas as it was the same film being transported from cinema to cinema. Because of this, all cinemas showed different films. Nowadays, there would be lots of copies of the same movie. One local theatre, The Belgrave, always got the films last and by then, they were worse for wear and quite often had bits missing.

Turning up to a film on time meant sitting through trailers for new films and plenty of Pearl and Dean adverts featuring cigarettes, chocolates and the local takeaway. If you missed the beginning of the film, you could always just sit through it again, nobody checked much in those days. If you were caught doing this by an usherette, all you had to say was that you'd missed the beginning and that was alright.

There was also a couple of Thunderbirds movies in the 1960s which every kid had to see. Thunderbirds was just about the best telly programme on at the time and we all loved it.

Planet of the Apes was one of our favourite films of the 1960s. I think we were probably too young to see it but we still got in. Back then, we didn't care if it was a beautiful sunny day and we were going to be sat inside, in the dark, watching a film. As a kid, I became engrossed in a film and, for the couple of hours it was on, felt part of it.

Going to the pictures was great fun. Even the adverts and the intervals with choc ices and hot dogs made it something special. Being a small boy, I absolutely loved Planet of the Apes and we all imitated them when we left the cinema!

A trip to the pictures was something magical in the 1960s and some of my favourite movies come from that time especially all the Disney films, James Bond and all time favourites like Doctor Doolittle and Chitty Chitty Bang Bang.

Eleven

Food and Household shopping

One of the first things you saw every morning was a cereal packet. Kids loved cereal mainly because of the free gifts inside the boxes which would include toy cars, badges, soldiers, spinning tops and model aeroplanes. The packets were all brightly coloured and featured characters from Star Trek, Thunderbirds, Sooty and Sweep, Tom and Jerry and Walt Disney's The Jungle Book.

One of the earliest set of gifts I can remember were given away in Kellogg's Sugar Smacks and included plastic models of yesteryear which included a penny-farthing, a double decker bus, a car, a train, a steam locomotive and a wagon. My favourite was the penny-farthing! As soon as we got the cereal home, it would be opened and the gift would be searched for! Sometimes, there would be disappointment because the machine packing them had missed the packet but other times it would work the other way, and there would be more than one free gift. The

Four badges from Star Trek which were given away free with Kellogg's Sugar Smacks.

most I ever found in a single box was five! Other favourite free gifts from the 1960s included Captain Scarlet badges, Star Trek badges, Thunderbird figures and model aeroplanes. The boxes were all made to appeal to children who would spend ages staring at them. The Sugar Smacks box with the Star Trek badges featured a drawing of Spock. We all saw them and they were instantly thrown in the bin when they were finished. Few people kept them and recently a Spock box came up for auction for several thousand pounds.

Kellogg's had their own Noddy club. By saving the packet tops and sending them away, you were sent a Noddy badge and certificate saying that you were in the Noddy Club.

Other memorable cereal boxes included characters from Thunderbirds. Tarzan, who had been made popular by the tv show featuring Ron Ely, appeared on boxes of Nabisco's Cubs (spoon sized Shredded Wheat). The cardboard jungle scene on the back of the box was used for the free rub-down Action transfers contained inside. Kellogg's Cornflakes boxes regularly had cardboard cut-outs on the back. These included masks of cowboys, Indians, pirates and other characters as well as members of the crew of Star Trek. There were also cut-out figures

and the ones that I best remember were from Orlando
O'Connor, a long-since forgotten tv show starring Sam
Kydd. The show starred Kydd, who played a smuggler,
and was aired between 1965 and 1968. Other popular cut-
outs on the back of cereal packets included puppets of the
characters from Jungle Book. Sugar Puffs had a
competition on the back of the pack to win a full size
Dalek! We entered but didn't win. I don't know how it
would have fitted into our small flat if we had won!
Every boy collected the tea cards from Brooke Bond and

A collection of Brooke Bond booklets containing cards saved from
boxes of tea.

there was as much excitement seeing which card was in the packet as there was with the free gifts in cereal. There were no tea bags back then and all tea came in a box. The cards made up sets which could be stuck in an album which cost 1 shilling. The sets included historical costumes, birds, flags, wild animals, trees, cars and many other subjects. There were always many doubles but these were swapped with friends at school.

All kids collected the paper golliwogs off Robertson jam and these could be sent away with one shilling to get either a golliwog statue or badge. As mentioned earlier, I remember our first golliwog coming in the post in a small cardboard box wrapped in straw. He was a clarinet player. He stood on the shelf before being knocked off and broken (he was soon fixed!).

Other products had things to appeal to kids. Heinz gave away free space posters and well as pictures to collect of dinosaurs on their labels. Findus gave away free flexi discs featuring the Apollo 11 moon landing and Crosse and Blackwell gave away stamps of the world which every young boy collected at the time.

The Magic Roundabout featured on the packets of Birds Instant Whip. Some had a colouring competition on the back which I entered and won when I was about 6 years old. The prize was a box of drawings and pens from the show to colour in. It seemed very exciting to me at the time!

NEW PICTURE CARDS!

Meet the Cock of the Rock—one of the
80 magnificent birds in the new
Brooke Bond series of
picture cards.*

COLLECT
BROOKE BOND
'TROPICAL
BIRDS'

SPECIAL ALBUM, TOO*

—to hold the complete set; full of extra
information. Price 6d from your grocer, or
send a 6d postal order to Brooke Bond Tea
Ltd., Dept. P.C., 35 Cannon Street,
London, E.C.4.
*Available in U.K. only.

**THERE'S A *FREE*
PICTURE CARD
IN ALL PACKETS OF
BROOKE BOND TEA**

We all enjoyed collecting Brooke Bond cards which featured sets
including trees, cars, fashion, butterflies and birds.

134

Most everyday shopping was bought from the local shop owned by a Mrs Crook who also sold American comics and sweets. There were plenty of little shops nearby where we could get everything we needed. Once a week, usually on a Saturday, we would catch the bus into town (it was packed in the days before pedestrianisation) and get anything we couldn't get locally. My favourite shop

Cereal toys given away free with Kellogg's Sugar Smacks.

was Woolworth's where everything we wanted seemed to be 6/6. I loved the toy section but they also sold allsorts of other stuff for the home. We'd usually end up having dinner in the same restaurant (everyone went there) before getting home for the wrestling at 4pm. Everyone rushed home for the wrestling back then but, if you were still in the shops as late as 4.30pm, a bell would ring to inform you that they would soon be closing.

Jackie Pallo, with his distinct blonde hair and pony tail, was one of the most popular wrestlers on tv in the 1960s and 1970s.

There were no major supermarkets which was just as well because most homes had nowhere to store endless amounts of food. People didn't have freezers and most families had a tiny fridge with a very small freezer compartment in the top which usually stored either a box of Birdseye fish fingers or a tub of ice cream which had been bought from the local van.

Most areas had their own corner shop which would sell all the essentials such as food, sweets and chocolate, newspapers, cigarettes and tobacco, cards and toys. Other nearby shops could include a newsagents, a butchers, a make and mend (for anyone into DIY), a post office, a wool shop (knitting was very popular), a clothes shop and the first British takeaway, the fish and chip shop!

Milk was delivered to the door by a milkman and everything that was needed that was essential could be bought nearby.

Buying food locally meant that everyone got to meet up and everyone knew each other. Everything you needed was to hand. It certainly seemed a friendlier time and nowadays, with bustling superstores and large shopping centres, all that seems to have disappeared.

Every 1960s household wanted the latest gadgets and technology including a fridge freezer. Most freezers were only big enough for a few items such as a tub of ice cream (bought off the ice cream man) and a packet of fish fingers!

Twelve

Comics and books

My favourite comics in the 1960s had to be The Beano
and The Dandy which we got delivered by the paper boy
every week. I used to take The Beano to school with me
and try and read it but would get fed up carrying it and
would hide it somewhere to collect later. Mrs Crook's
shop across the way also sold American comics. Tarzan
was very popular so I read those but probably my
favourite were Batman and Superman.
Alan read comics such as Valiant, Hurricane and Tiger
which all featured adventure-type stories. Sometimes we
would get TV Century 21 because we all loved Doctor
Who, Stingray, Thunderbirds, Captain Scarlet and Joe 90.
We were all attracted by the free gifts that were offered
with comics. Things like toy planes, badges, jokes and
sweets were given away. The Joe 90 comic had a cut out
car and featured comic strips of Land of the Giants
(which everyone loved), Star Trek and The Champions. It

We all loved pirates and also loved the Valiant comic so a combination of both was an excellent idea. The Valiant Book of Pirates came out in 1967.

140

was a companion comic for the extremely popular TV21 and outsold it for many weeks. Joe 90 was one of the most watched programmes and anything associated with it was bound to sell. In September 1969, TV21 and the Joe 90 comic merged but still kept all the best-loved strips which were excellently drawn with many in colour. Other popular comics of the time included the pocket-sized Commando which featured grim war stories. Alan read it but I preferred something more like the Beano. War stories were very popular at the time and, even though it was the 1960s, most of us still had the same dislike of Germans that people had 20 years before. This was probably kept going by films and dramas on the tv and most of our breaks at school would be spent running around pretending to machine gun each other! We all knew a few words of German from these comics, mainly 'Achtung!', 'Swinehund!' and 'Heil Hitler!' - none of which came in handy when I took German at Secondary School (I failed the exam!).

Buster was another favourite comic that we loved. Amazingly, it ran from 1960 until 2000! When the comic was released in 1960, an advert in the Daily Mirror announced that Buster was the son of their own comic strip character, Andy Capp. The first issue, out on 23rd May 1960, had the all important free gift which was a 'Balloon Bleeper!'. The free gift with Issue 2

One of the best comics of the 1960s, if you liked tv science fiction, was TV Century 21 which featured all our favourites including Doctor Who, Thunderbirds and Captain Scarlet.

142

was a 'Zoomer Jet' which you whizzed around your head on a piece of string. Issue 3 gave away a 'Fool 'Em All Dodger Kit' which consisted of a false nose, moustache and glasses! The comic cost 4d.

Other favourite comics of the time included POW, Wham and Giggle.

American comics had many weird and wonderful adverts selling things like Sea Monkeys, X-Ray specs and Charles Atlas' bodybuilding course. The advert for Sea Monkeys showed them in their bowl reading newspapers and watching the telly. Some would be doing gymnastics. If you managed to get hold of some Sea Monkeys what you actually got was a packet full of powder which you poured into water and waited. After about a few weeks, small shrimps would hatch out. Nothing like monkeys or the things in the advert and certainly none of them ever watched the telly or read newspapers.

X-Ray specs were equally as disappointing. The advert showed that you could see the bones in your hands or see through people's clothes. They consisted of a piece of cardboard with two holes in. In the holes were two feathers like the kind you'd find in a pillow. For some reason, this gave the effect that you could see through things (although it wasn't very good).

The advert for Charles Atlas' Bodybuilding kit seemed an odd thing to put in a comic. I didn't know another 7 year old who wanted to have a body like Charles Atlas (he'd been dead for 30 years!). I suppose they thought that anyone who read a Superman comic might want to build themselves up to look like their hero. It never happened.

Most of these send-away gifts in American comics were unobtainable to us and we only heard about them through kids whose dads were in the Navy and they'd lived there. Most of the adverts wouldn't send stuff outside the US although I did write to Archie Comics and they sent me a membership card and badge (which I wore to school instead of my 'house' badge - the Deputy Headmaster wasn't impressed!).

Many British comics linked up with tv programmes and featured many strips from Gerry Anderson shows. TV21 was a favourite comic with many boys and featured Stingray, Fireball XL5 and Supercar. The cover of the copy on page 142 features the stuff of every boys' nightmares - a Dalek!

A selection of annuals from the 1960s including Joe 90, The Flintstones, Atom Ant, Dr Who, The Monkees and TV21.

144

Every August, we'd look forward to mum's shopping catalogue arriving. It was a big heavy thing from Great Universal, Janet Frazer or Freeman's and you could pay things up over 20 weeks. As soon as the catalogue arrived, we'd flick straight to the toy section and see what annuals were coming out for Christmas. There was an excitement on the build up to Christmas, waiting to see what annuals we got and to see what our favourite cartoon characters were up to.

There were certainly some excellent and fantastic comics out in the 1960s and I wish that I'd kept them all!

The very first book we were given to read at school was the very politically incorrect, 'The Little Black Sambo'. Nowadays, there would be an uproar if such a book appeared on the school syllabus (although it's still available today). As a small boy, I didn't see it as being racist at all and all kids enjoyed reading it at the time. Other books we were given to read included Janet and John and various Ladybird books which covered all subjects including history, transport, fairy tales, religion, nursery rhymes, famous people as well as many more. We loved them all but soon discovered Enid Blyton. There wasn't a kid in the class who hadn't read The Famous Five or The Secret Seven. The Secret Seven contained characters such as Fatty and Loony which seem to have disappeared from later editions. The Three Golliwogs included the main characters Golly, Woggy and Nigger. The last copy of the book seems to have been published in 1970 before later being republished, with different character names, as The Three Gollies. We all loved these books when we were kids and none of us were racist but today, they'd be frowned upon.

Other books we enjoyed included books featuring Noddy, Rupert, Bill and Ben and Andy Pandy.

Later, I discovered CS Lewis's The Lion, the Witch and the Wardrobe and became engrossed in the Narnia series. For a while, I seemed to be constantly reading and read all sorts of mystery and adventure books. There was something far more thrilling reading the story in a book than there ever was watching it on the tv or as a film. Perhaps one day, I'll read them all again!

Thirteen

Music

The first record I remember ever hearing on the radio,
when I was a little boy, was Downtown by Petula Clark.
I was three years old and we were packing to leave from
Weymouth to Singapore. While it was playing, I was
eating chocolate buttons from a toy tin post box and
playing with a tin flying saucer. It's funny how you
remember specific songs that were playing at eventful
times in your life. I'll always remember Please Release
Me by Englebert Humpidinck because it was playing
when I cracked my head open on a window when I was
about 5 and I'll always remember Yellow Submarine by
The Beatles because it was playing while one of my
dad's naval friends was giving a firework display and a
Catherine Wheel flew up one of the legs of his shorts!
For most of the beginning of the 1960s, all our music
came from the radio and we didn't have a record player
for a long time after that.

Although The Beatles provided much of the music for the 1960s, being a small boy at the time, I almost missed out on them completely and the only song that sticks in my mind is Yellow Submarine, probably because of the cartoon, which no-one understood, and the brightly coloured Corgi toy that was brought out at the same time. My parents had a reel-to-reel tape recorder that they

brought back from Singapore and they had a few tapes including the Black and White Minstrels, Carousel, The Sound of Music and South Pacific. It wasn't until 1969 that we had our first record player which was a Dansette-type player that you could stack your records up on and they would play one after another.

We had very few records and I think the first single we owned was 'Sugar, Sugar' by The Archies. Alan probably bought this one as the first single I can remember buying was 'Wandrin' Star' by Lee Marvin. We used to play it at

78 rpm and I remember one time doing this and we couldn't stop laughing. We were easily pleased!

Our next door neighbour had a pile of singles that he gave us so that was our record collection. One of the singles was 'A Little Bit Me, A Little Bit You' by the Monkees and I became a fan of theirs soon after. I think the only LP I had for a long time was a Music For Pleasure copy of The Monkees Greatest Hits.

Every Saturday, Alan and me would venture into town to the old record store in the market and either buy second-hand records or swap any old ones we had (we never got a very good deal). Very soon, I had every one of the

Some of our favourite records of the 1960s including The Rolling Stones, The Monkees. The Beatles, Simon and Garfunkel and Elvis Presley.

149

Monkees' LPs and listened to them over and over. While in town, we would also visit the second-hand book store and buy annuals, some of which we took apart and stuck on the wall. For a while, I had The Monkees everywhere. Of course, we had my dad's reel-to-reel tape recorder so we'd tape the Top 40 every week. The microphone picked up every sound so if we wanted a good recording, everyone had to keep quiet (which hardly ever happened!)

Hearing The Archies sing 'Sugar, Sugar' takes me straight back to the autumn of 1969. Hearing 'In the Year 2525' by Zager and Evans reminds me of the summer of that year, building dens, racing push bikes, playing on building sites and just generally getting up to mischief. We'd also tape Top of the Pops when we could but Alan Freeman's Top 40 show was the best place to get the latest tunes.

Many shops had their own record departments. We'd wander down to the Co-op or to Boots in town just to listen to records in the specially made booths they had there. Every booth had a pair of head phones and you could ask to hear any record you liked. It's funny how entertainment has changed over the years!

Dialling 16 on the telephone would get you a latest chart hit and the service was very popular for many years. In later years, we'd always wait until mum and dad had gone out, usually in the school holidays, before phoning up. Most kids would go to the local phone box to hear their favourite tunes.

Of course, we'd always had a radio and the songs that

really remind me of the previous year (1968) when we lived at Devonport were 'The Ballad of Bonnie and Clyde' by Georgie Fame, 'Cinderella Rockefella' by Esther and Abi Ofarim (I can remember my mum singing it), 'Congratulations' by Cliff Richard, 'Lily the Pink' by The Scaffold and 'Those Were the Days' by Mary Hopkin.

We all loved watching Opportunity Knocks and Mary Hopkin shot to fame by appearing on it.

'I Love Jennifer Eccles' by The Hollies which was a hit in March 1968 always reminds me of our Easter holiday while we lived at Devonport.

There was something special about saving up to buy an LP. Once you had it in your hands, you would read every part of the cover on the bus home and again in your bedroom as you played the record. Something was lost when LPs disappeared and CDs took over. There was something wonderful about a 12 inch album cover that was very appealing. Cassettes also lacked the appeal of a vinyl LP.

A portable Dansette record player.

Fourteen

Holidays

School holidays were much looked forward to. We had 3 weeks off at Easter, 6 weeks in the Summer and 2 weeks at Christmas. In the Spring, the weather was good enough to go out playing in the woods, looking for birds' nests and tadpoles and generally exploring. Summer holidays were a time for building dens and go-karts, playing football and generally being outdoors. Christmas holidays were very exciting with the prospect of presents, Christmas dinner and extra television programmes. It was a lot colder but we still managed to get out and explore the area.

Holidays abroad throughout most of the 1960s were unheard of and no-one from my class took a holiday overseas. The most exotic place you could go was to one of the many Butlin's holiday camps throughout the UK. Even then, most families couldn't afford to go but we all enjoyed listening to other kids' stories about their holidays there. We finally went to Butlin's in Clacton in 1970. I loved it!

During the 1960s, our only holiday away from home was, as I mentioned earlier, staying in a caravan at Challaborough in Devon. We were right beside the sea and in a cramped caravan, with no telly or much else, it seemed great fun to me! Even staying indoors listening to the rain hit the tin roof seemed a good time. Reading Enid Blyton books and watching similar programmes at home on the telly every day, the holiday seemed like an adventure where we could meet smugglers, escaped convicts or find hidden treasure. Of course, none of it happened but being a 7 year old in the 1960s, it felt like it could. Having a great imagination was all that was needed to have a good time.

We all looked forward to our school holidays and counted the days until the next ones. Summer holidays seemed to go on forever and there always seemed to be lots of sunshine. Easter time and during the summer, the fair would come to town. We'd get taken by our parents and my favourite ride was always the dodgems. We'd always go out of our way to bump as many cars as we could (as did all the kids). Occasionally, we'd end up driving the wrong way and would be told off. There was always some bloke working in the fairground who would give you the wrong change (or no change) and they were so rough looking, that half the time you didn't ask for it! We also loved going on the Big Wheel. You had to be a certain height to go on it but most of the time, it didn't seem to matter. Another favourite ride was the Cyclone which seemed to just miss the central post every time it went by it. We also went on the Noah's Ark but avoided the Waltzer. If the scary fairground bloke spun you

154

around too many times, you were sure to be sick. We loved the slot machines and the machines where you put in a halfpenny to try and get it to slide behind a mountain of other halfpennies to try to knock them over the edge. There was definitely a knack to it as there was with the 'grabbit' machine. It seemed impossible to win anything let alone the big prizes. There were also hoopla games (I'm sure it was also impossible) and a tin duck shoot which Alan and dad were good at but I wasn't. I think we won a nodding lion toy which sat on the back shelf of the car until all its fur fell off. The sun must have got to it!

A souvenir badge from a trip to see the Lions of Longleat.

Having a car meant that we could take a trip to Longleat. All the kids at school would talk about it especially the monkeys ripping off windscreen wipers and wing mirrors!
We went, saw the lions which didn't do much and wound the windows up quickly when the monkeys attacked. Our

car came out intact but many of the monkeys had enough spare parts from other vehicles to build their own car! Holiday times were mainly just playing outside in the sun (the sun shone back then!), having adventures, building dens and lying in the long grass and ferns staring at the sky until it was tea time. Once tea was over, we were straight out again until it got dark.

It always seemed a let down having to go back to school after the holidays had finished. I'd always daydream about what I'd been doing the same time the week before and would count down the days until the next school break!

Towards the end of the 1960s, package holidays were introduced to various places including Spain. Some families travelled abroad instead of the usual holidays within Britain. However, when I was a boy, it seemed very uncommon for anyone to take their holidays overseas.

A Butlin's badge from Skegness from 1961.

Fifteen

Technology

To me, as a boy, the greatest thing that happened during the 1960s was when Neil Armstrong became the first man on the moon. Every kid was excited and it was the main topic of conversation at school. We were allowed to watch the moonwalk at school on the black and white television in the hall and afterwards we all walked like spacemen in the playground. For a while, cowboys and Indians and war games were forgotten as we all became astronauts. Jumping off the school roof or nearby garages and pretending to land like a spaceman seemed great fun for a while but gravity always ruined it and I'm sure that some boys ended up with broken arms. We all had space toys including models of astronauts, Apollo rockets and lunar modules. Some kids even had their own space helmets which could be bought from Woolworths. For many of us, the closest we thought that we would come to weightlessness was by bouncing around on a

The crew of the Apollo 11 mission showing Neil Armstrong, Michael Collins and Buzz Aldrin.

Spacehopper which became a craze towards the end of the 1960s and the beginning of the 1970s. They were never as exciting as they looked on the telly but that didn't stop us bouncing all over the place!

At school, there were extra tv programmes, explaining all, usually hosted by Patrick Moore. We all had space posters all over our walls and many of us got our mums to buy us the Observer book of Astronomy by Patrick Moore.

For a while, everything went space crazy. There were bubblegum cards of the moon project (which we all collected and swapped in the playground), Brooke Bond released Race Into Space cards later in the early 1970s and Walls Ice Cream also produced cards while Lyons Maid issued astronaut badges which had to be sent away for by saving the tokens from popular ice lollies. Anything to do with the moon and space was suddenly very popular although boys had always enjoyed the many science fiction tv series that were on at the time such as Lost in Space, Star Trek, The Invaders, Land of the Giants and, later in 1970, Gerry Anderson's UFO.

Cassette players came out in the 1960s but most kids at our school didn't have one until the early 1970s. Many got one as a reward for passing the 11+. Cassettes were an alternative to vinyl LPs but both were produced side by side and no-one ever thought that the cassette would take over from the LP or vinyl 7 inch singles.

Amazingly, there were lots of things invented in the 1960s that you wouldn't expect, although most of us didn't have them until decades later. These included the first audio cassette (1962), the first computer video game (also 1962), the first video disk (1965), the first CD (1965), the first handheld calculator (1967), the computer mouse (1968) and the barcode scanner (1969). Other 1960s inventions included the first fibre tip pens, acrylic paint, astroturf, contact lenses, fuel injection for cars, the first computer with integrated circuits, RAM memory and the artificial heart. Most of these inventions had little impact on a kid living in the 1960s.

Buzz Aldrin on the surface of the moon. The reflection of Neil
Armstrong, who took the photo, can be seen reflected in his visor.

The thing that we were most fascinated with was the television which only showed black and white programmes and had to be re-tuned by hand, together with lots of crackling, if you wanted to view the other side. At the time, nobody had ever seen a remote control or knew anybody who had a colour set. Tv's were affected a lot by 'ghosting' and someone would have to try every position they could with the table top aerial to get a decent picture. Some people had roof top aerials but these still suffered from shadows and ghosting.
Most new technology revolved around the kitchen with things like electric kettles that could turn themselves off, washing machines, modern cookers, electric irons and larger fridges.
Transistor radios were invented in the 1950s but didn't really come into popular use until the 1960s and 1970s. For the first time, a radio was small enough to fit in your pocket. Inventive kids took them to school and had an earplug running behind their ear back to the radio so they could listen in class. Transistor radios sold in their billions in the 1960s and 1970s although it wasn't until the middle 1970s that most kids had one of their own.

Sixteen

Cars and transport

My parents had several cars during the 1960s. The first that I can remember was a grey Ford Prefect which had the registration number WXW 916. Dad paid £147 for it in about 1962 and we had it until we left for Singapore in 1965.

It was rare during the 1960s for people to have a car and I remember in the later 1960s how our street was so empty of passing traffic that we'd play football in the road. One kid, for a joke, lay down in the road and waited for a car to come along. I think he'd seen someone do it on the telly. It sounds dangerous nowadays but what actually happened at the time was that he got so fed up waiting for a car to come along that he gave up on his prank and we all carried on playing football.

There certainly was traffic around, just not on the scale that there is today. I remember one boy running out in traffic up by the shops and not looking and he was hit by a car and thrown in the air. There certainly seemed to be more near misses then than there are now (even though people nowadays seem to have less road sense).

Public information films would warn children of the dangers of traffic and warn them not to step out behind an ice cream van or bus or from between parked cars. The main adverts featured Tufty the squirrel (or Tufty Fluffytail). Tufty was the idea of Elsie Mills MBE who created safety stories for The Royal Society for the Prevention of Accidents. Tufty first saw the light of day in 1953 and by 1961, the Tufty Club was launched for under fives. By the early 1970s, there were over 2 million members and the campaign continued into the 1980s.

In the 1960s, most people were happy catching the bus. If there was a car in the family, dad would use it to go to work or it might just be used for special journeys or days out. By the later 1960s, there were more cars about and days to the seaside in the summer (or anywhere else) would mean sitting in a mile-long traffic jam. Roads were less comprehensive and traffic soon became congested. Often a pedestrian could walk past traffic on a hot day and get to his destination long before a car could.

By the end of the decade, petrol was about five shillings (25p) a gallon.

I remember the smell of the leather seats in the early cars of the 1960s. Some had the luxury of walnut dashboards. For a while, we had a Triumph Herald and I can still remember everything about that car especially when we were going out on an outing on a sunny day.

We both loved it when dad pulled into the garage mainly

Me sat on our old grey Ford Prefect at Weymouth in about 1964.

because of the free gifts! Garages weren't self-service back then and as soon as you pulled onto the forecourt, someone would come out and ask you how much petrol you wanted. Some garages, such as Shell, would check your oil, water and tyre pressures and even clean your windscreen. Petrol for many years was below five shillings (25p) a gallon. After you'd paid, all without getting out of the car, a man would return with your

Esso 'Put a Tiger in your Tank' free badges. We all loved going to Esso garages for the free gifts.

change and various free gifts. Every kid loved the Tiger campaign at the Esso garages and the free gifts included tiger tails (ideal for your bike), badges, glasses and beakers, stuffed toys, stickers and many other items. Shell also had many gifts including 3D animal stickers as well as tumblers and other nonsense that only adults would want. Esso won hands down getting kids to pester their parents to pull into their garages for enticing free gifts!

The 1960s had some very memorable cars including the Ford Cortina. The Cortina was first made in 1962 and by the 1970s, it was Britain's best-selling car.

If you were well-off, the car to have was an E-Type Jaguar which came out in 1961 and cost an incredible £2,197. In comparison, the average cost of a house in 1961 was £2, 770! There certainly weren't any E-Type Jags where we lived although one young couple in the street owned a white Lotus. Sports cars stood out in the 1960s as most people, if they owned a car at all, had a car suited towards their family. There were some very sporty cars available in the 1960s and many are fondly remembered but most were seen mainly on the television being driven by people like The Saint! Sought after sports cars included the Porsche 911, the Triumph TR4, The Austin Healey Frogeye Sprite, the MGB and, of course, Simon Templar's car, the Volvo P1800. As a kid, I don't remember seeing any sports cars on the streets (other than our neighbours' Lotus). By the late 1960s, dad had a second-hand blue Vauxhall Viva which was comparable to the Ford Cortina. Unfortunately, it broke down regularly.

167

Puzzle books and I-Spy books were ideal for a long car journey.

Many cars in those days were second-hand and it seemed unusual for someone to have a brand new car. The cars on the road at the time stretched back many years and there were some real classics out and about.

Many cars in the later 1960s had seat belts but many people didn't wear them and there were no rear seatbelts for kids or passengers.

Police cars were often Ford Cortinas in blue and white. These patrol cars became known as Panda cars. Other popular cars used by the police included Morris Minors and Ford Anglias.

Amazingly, cars such as the MG Roadster were used for traffic duties and, in the early 1960s, for patrolling the newly-built motorways.

Many police cars where we lived were Morris Minors or Austin 1100s. All made the familiar 'Nee-Nah' sound when driving to an emergency. It's funny that kids still

A tiger tail given away free with Esso petrol. They were much sought after by boys who either tied them to their bikes or to their dad's wing mirror.

make this noise today even though police cars have a totally different sound.

All buses were double-deckers and all were very well-used by people travelling to work or to the town. All buses had a driver and a conductor and you would take your seat before the conductor came around with his ticket machine shouting 'tickets please!'. The fares weren't very dear, perhaps a couple of pennies. As kids, we would ask the driver or conductor for a roll of tickets which we would then unroll and run home with them flying behind us. All kids did it.

Sitting upstairs with your mum on the bus was an adventure. Making sure that you could sit by the window seemed great fun. Smoking was still allowed on buses back then and there would always be some teenagers at the back of the bus, swearing (it seems tame nowadays) and puffing cigarettes. Mums would always be telling them off saying things like 'there's kids on board' and that would usually be enough for them to quieten down. Sometimes the conductor would tell them off or even throw them off and make them walk home. The seats came in purple leatherette material and were generally vandalised. When you reached your stop, you'd ring the bell and the driver would open the door (sometimes too early). Most people thanked the driver before they got off.

There were many other vehicles on the roads at the time all of which appealed to children including fire engines, ambulances and steam rollers. Long journeys travelling on holiday, or for days out at the beach, meant taking our

I-Spy books. Motorways were quite empty of traffic and stories of people safely doing u-turns weren't unheard of. Many people drove themselves but many caught a coach or train. For most of the 1960s, there were still steam trains although they had ran alongside diesel locomotives for many years. The last steam train service ran in Britain on 11th August 1968.

By the end of the 1960s, transport had changed greatly. There were many newer, faster roads together with many more sleek, stylish cars and other vehicles. Steam trains had gone forever, as had many railway lines. Far more families now owned a car and were able to travel further afield both to work and on holiday. Cars were no longer just available to the well-off and were now available to the masses.

Corgi's range of excellent racing cars. My dad's cars never looked like any of these!

Seventeen

A Boy's View of
World Events

I'd be lying if I said, as a boy, that I was affected by many of the world events that took place in the 1960s apart from the moon landings.

When you're a boy, out enjoying yourself building dens or getting up to other mischief, world events pass you by. I remember our junior school teacher asking if we watched the news on tv or read the papers. Nobody showed any interest. The only things that we found interesting in the papers were the tv page (my favourite), the cartoons at the back and, if your parents got the Sun, the page 3 girl!

Amazingly, stories like the assassination of John F Kennedy (and later Robert F Kennedy), the Great Train Robbery, Nelson Mandela's imprisonment, the assassination of Martin Luther King and Malcolm X, the first heart transplant, the Vietnam War and the death of Che Guevara passed me by!

Although there were events during the 1960s that affected me such as the first James Bond movie (1962), the first showing of Dr Who (1963) and the beginning of Star Trek (1966) and other favourite tv programmes.
Dr Who seemed marvellous (and scary) when it first appeared on our screens starring William Hartnell. There was something very reminiscent of German Stormtroopers when the Daleks were first shown and

John F Kennedy and Jackie Kennedy in Dallas, Texas on 22nd November 1963 seconds before he was assassinated.

their appearance must have given boys nightmares up and down the land. I loved the show especially when Patrick Troughton took over and then we were scared all over again by Cybermen!

Star Trek seemed very futuristic and even things like doors opening on their own seemed amazing.

James Bond's first appearance in Dr No caught every child's imagination but it wasn't until Goldfinger that all the merchandise seemed to take off and every boy had his own Corgi DB5 or spy sets. What was strange was that most boys were far to young to even get into the cinema to see the film although they had all seemed to have seen it. We went with our parents in 1964. I think I fell asleep although I was only 3 years old at the time!

My world revolved around the area near to my home - the woods, the building site and school. Television (although not the news), films and books fuelled my imagination. The great thing about being a boy is that you haven't got all the worries you have when you're an adult and everything you need, including your friends and family, are close by.

World events no doubt had an effect on our parents, their friends and our teachers but our only worry was where we were going to build our new den, what was on the telly and what we were having for tea!

Anyway, the next chapter deals with the most memorable events of the 1960s!

Martin Luther King in 1964.

Eighteen

Memorable events of the 1960s

1960 : The Farthing is taken out of circulation on 31st December.

1961 : John F Kennedy becomes the 35th president of the United States on 20th January.

1961 : Yuri Gagarin becomes the first man in space on 12th April.

1961 : Alan Shepard becomes the first American in space on 5th May.

1961 : The Berlin wall is constructed commencing on 13th August.

1962 : John Glenn becomes the first American to orbit the Earth on 20th February.

1962 : AT & T's Telstar becomes the first communications satellite to be launched into space on 10th July.

1962 : The first audio cassette is invented.

1962 : The first live transatlantic television is broadcast via the Telstar Satellite 0n 23rd July.

1962 : Marilyn Monroe is found dead on 5th August.

Marilyn Monroe and Jane Russell outside Grauman's Chinese Theatre on 26th June 1953.

1963 : Doctor Who is first broadcast on 23rd November. It stars William Hartnell as the Doctor.

1963 : The Beatles have their first number one hit. Their first album, 'Please Please Me' is released on 22nd March.

1963 : Dr No is released.

1963 : John F Kennedy is assassinated on 22nd November.

1963 : The Great Train Robbery takes place in Buckinghamshire on 8th August.

1963 : Martin Luther King delivers his famous speech featuring the words, 'I have a dream' on the steps of the Lincoln Memorial on 28th August.

1964 : BBC2 is first broadcast on 20th April.

1964 : The Beatles arrive at JFK International airport and are met by thousands of fans marking the first occasion of Beatlemania in America.

1964 : Cassius Clay beats Sonny Liston to be crowned Heavyweight Champion of the World in Florida on 25th February.

1964 : On 15th March, Elizabeth Taylor and Richard Burton marry for the first time.

1964 : On 29th March, Radio Caroline becomes the first pirate station to broadcast to the mainland from a ship anchored outside Britain's territorial waters.

1964 : On the 4th April, The Beatles hold the top 5 positions in the US Billboard chart with Can't Buy Me Love, Twist and Shout, She Loves You, I Want to Hold your Hand and Please Please Me.

1964: On 8th April, Gemini 1 is launched.

1964 : From Russia With Love is released on 8th April.

1964 : On 16th April, the Rolling Stones release their first album.

1964 : On 12th June, Nelson Mandela is sentence to life imprisonment in South Africa.

1964 : On 31st July, Ranger 7 sends back the first close-up pictures of the moon.

1964 : On 27th August, Walt Disney's Mary Poppins is released in America.

1964 : On 17th September, Goldfinger is first released.

1964 : Bewitched is aired for the first time in America on 17th September.

Bewitched is one of the best remembered comedies of the
1960s. It starred Elizabeth Montgomery, Dick York and Agnes
Moorehead as Samantha, Darrin and Endora.

1964 : The Kinks first album is released on 2nd October.

1964 : On 14th October, Martin Luther King wins the Nobel Peace Prize.

1964 : On 16th October, Harold Wilson becomes the Prime Minister of Great Britain.

1964 : Wonderful Radio London begins transmitting from a ship anchored off the south coast of England on 23rd December.

1965 : Winston Churchill dies on 24th January.

1965 : The Sound of Music opens in New York on 2nd March.

1965 : Cosmonaut Aleksei Leonov becomes the first man to walk in space on 18th March.

1965 : Astronaut Edward Higgins makes the first American space walk, leaving Gemini 4, on 3rd June.

1965 : Cigarette advertising is banned on British tv on 1st August.

1965 : The Tom and Jerry cartoon series makes its first appearance on US television on 25th September.

Winston Churchill giving his famous V for Victory greeting on 20th
May 1940.

1966 : Indira Gandhi is elected Prime Minister of India on 24th January.

1966 : The Soviet Luna 9 becomes the first controlled rocket-assisted spacecraft to land on the Moon.

1966 : The FIFA World Cup trophy is stolen on 20th June and is found, wrapped in newspaper, seven days later by a dog called Pickles.

1966 : The Labour Party led by Harold Wilson wins the General Election on 31st March.

1966 : A regular hovercraft service begins across the English Channel on 30th April.

1966 : *Swinging Radio England* and *Britain Radio* commence broadcasting on 3rd May from a ship anchored off the south coast of England.

1966 : Pet Sounds is released by The Beach Boys on 16th May.

1966 : England wins the World Cup after beating West Germany 4-2 on 30th July.

1966 : Star Trek makes its debut on 8th September in America.

1966 : Patrick Troughton takes over the role of Doctor Who from William Hartnell on 29th October.

1966 : Walt Disney dies while producing The Jungle Book on 15th December.

1967 : US astronauts Gus Grissom, Edward Higgins White and Roger Chaffee are killed when fire breaks out during a launch pad test of Apollo 1 on 27th January.

1967 : Puppet on a String sung by Sandie Shaw wins the Eurovision Song Contest on 8th April.

1967 : Elvis Presley marries Priscilla Beaulieu in Las Vegas on 1st May.

1967 : BBC2 is the first UK channel to broadcast in colour on 1st July.

1967 : Brian Epstein, the manager of the Beatles, is found dead in his bedroom on 27th August.

1967 : The BBC's Light Programme is split and becomes Radio 1 and Radio 2 on 30th September.

1967 : The first heart transplant takes place on 3rd December.

1968 : 2001 : A Space Odyssey premieres in America on 2nd April.

Robert F Kennedy in 1964.

1968 : Planet of the Apes starring Charlton Heston is released on 3rd April.

1968 : Martin Luther King is shot dead in Memphis, Tennessee on 4th April.

1968 : Robert F Kennedy is assassinated in Los Angeles on 5th June.

1968 : Mattel's Hot Wheels toy cars are released on 6th September.

1968 : The tv show Hawaii 5-0 debuts in America on 20th September.

1968 : NASA launches the first manned Apollo mission, Apollo 7. The first live broadcast from orbit takes place.

1968 : The White Album is released by the Beatles on 22nd November.

1969 : Richard Nixon becomes 37th President of the United States on 20th January.

1969 : The Beatles give their last public performance on the roof of Apple Records on 30th January.

1969 : Two cosmonauts leave Soyuz 5 for Soyuz 4 and become the first men to transfer between two spacecraft.

Richard Nixon, the 37th President of the United States.

1969: The Boeing 747 makes its maiden flight on 9th February.

1969 : Concorde makes its first test flight on 2nd March.

1969 : Apollo 9 is launched to test the Lunar Module on 3rd March.

1969 : Golda Meir becomes the first female Prime Minister of Israel on 17th March.

1969 : John Lennon and Yoko Ono marry in Gibraltar on 20th March.

1969 : Robert Knox-Johnson becomes the first man to sail around the world single-handed on 22nd April.

1969 : Apollo 10 is launched on 18th May, a rehearsal for the moon landing.

1969 : Judy Garland dies of a drug overdose on 22nd June.

1969 : Charles becomes the Prince of Wales at Caernarfon on 1st July.

1969 : Brian Jones of the Rolling Stones drowns in a swimming pool at his home in Sussex on 3rd July.

Neil Armstrong became the first man on the moon on 21st July 1969.
His first words on the moon were, 'That's one small step for man, one
giant leap for mankind.'

1969 : US troops begin to withdraw from Vietnam on 8th July.

1969 : Apollo 11 lifts off for the moon on 16th July. On board are Neil Armstrong, Buzz Aldrin and Michael Collins.

1969 : The Lunar Module, Eagle, lands on the surface of the Moon on 20th July. Approximately 500 million people worldwide watch the live broadcast of Neil Armstrong taking the first steps on the Moon.

1969 : The Apollo 11 astronauts return safely from the Moon on 24th July.

1969 : The halfpenny ceases to be legal tender in Great Britain on 31st July,

1969 : The Beatles are photographed by Iain Macmillan on the zebra crossing at Abbey Road on 8th August.

1969 : The first ever episode of Scooby-Doo, Where are You is broadcasted in the US on 13th September.

1969 : Monty Python's Flying Circus is first aired on BBC2 on 5th October.

1969 : Sesame Street is first broadcast in the US on 10th November.

1969 : Apollo 12 is launched on 14th November, the second mission to the Moon. On board are astronauts Pete Conrad, Richard Gordon and Alan Bean.

1969 : Regular colour broadcasts begin on BBC 1 and ITV on 15th November.

1969 : Apollo 12 lands on the Moon on 19th November.

1969 : Pele scores his 1,000th goal on 19th November.

1969 : The Apollo 12 mission arrives safely back on Earth on 24th November.

1969 : John Lennon returns his MBE as a protest against Britain's involvement in the Nigerian Civil War.

Nineteen

Christmas

The one time of the year that children really looked forward to was Christmas. Mum would get us advent calendars and we'd open a door every day. This made the anticipation of Christmas far more exciting. Decorations would always go up 6 days before Christmas (not in October like nowadays!) and would come down 6 days after Christmas.

At school, there was much excitement with the Christmas Fete and the Nativity Play which we'd all take part in one way or another. I wasn't one of the actors but I remember we all helped out to make the stage decorations. Mr Smith lets us make Christmas cards in class and also showed us how to make 3-D stars out of card for the top of our trees. I was very impressed by them back then. On the last day of the term, we would be allowed to play games and bring in a toy. The classroom was decorated by bits of tinsel and paper chains that we'd made

Some of the wonderful toys available from Corgi in 1967 including the Daktari camouflaged Land Rover and 'Black Beauty' from Green Hornet. The show was banned in the UK because of its violence.

ourselves out of coloured paper.

We were read Bible stories about Jesus and the three wise men which we all absolutely loved although very few of us were religious in any way. In the assembly hall we would sing hymns such as 'Away in a Manger', 'Oh Little Town of Bethlehem', 'Once in Royal David's City' and 'Silent Night'. Looking back on it now, it was a magical and wonderous time and we were all very excited about what we were going to get for Christmas. Some of us were in the choir so going to church and singing hymns for the congregation also added to the magic of it all. At the end of term, we would have an assembly at the end of the day and the headmaster would wish us all a happy Christmas. The Christmas break seemed a long time when I was a kid but it was only about three weeks. Television played a big part in our enjoyment of Christmas. We'd all look forward to the Christmas copies of the Radio Times and TV Times coming out and would enjoy reading through them to see what was on over the holidays. There were always cartoons featuring Santa as well as lovely films such as 'It's a Wonderful Life', 'White Christmas" and 'Miracle on 34th Street'. Many of the films we all enjoyed were quite old at the time. Christmas shows featured Morecambe and Wise, Rolf Harris, Jimmy Tarbuck and Julie Andrews presenting Disney Time. In 1969, as well as the Queen's speech, there was also Top of the Pops, Billy Smart's Circus and Christmas Night with the Stars. The main feature film at 9.15 pm on BBC 1 was McLintock, a Western starring John Wayne. The lead up to Christmas was just as exciting as the actual day. For most of the 1960s, I still actually believed in Santa Claus so that added to the excitement.

By the time we'd broken up from school, mum would have put the decorations up and we'd all have decorated the tree. I always remember our tree being massive but looking at photos of it today, it appears quite small. For a few days leading up to Christmas, we'd make a bit of money by singing Christmas Carols at people's doors. All the kids would do it although I was never too keen. Alan would persuade me to go along, he probably saw some money in it because I was in the choir. We'd knock at the person's door and then at the last moment, Alan would run off leaving me there to sing on my own! Sometimes there would be a group of us doing it and once the choir from school went door to door singing to raise funds for the church.

Before Christmas, I'd write a note to Santa telling him what I wanted and would always get a reply. For anyone who doesn't know, he has writing very similar to my mum's!

I remember lying in our bunk beds and Alan telling me a Christmas story and asking if I could hear Santa's sleighbells. The more I listened, the more I could hear them. It wouldn't be until years later that I'd realise that the ringing in my ears was actually the beginning of tinnitus! Mum had already hung up our stockings at the end of the bed and we'd left some milk for Santa and a biscuit for Rudolph downstairs. I'd try my best to stay away so I could actually see Santa but always fell asleep.

Amazing price reductions on all Tommy Gunn equipment!

Equipment suitable
for all fighting soldiers!
Get a load of this: Battle pack price
cut from 19/11d to 13/11d! Trooping the
Colour pack used to cost 29/11d. Now it's
22/11d. And all Tommy Gunn
accessories such as Steel Helmet &
Foliage and Rifle now cost
under 4/-! Report to your shop and
build up your armoury at
lower cost. Remember:
Tommy Gunn equipment is
suitable for all fighting soldiers

A *Pedigree* PRODUCT

All boys loved toy soldiers and Pedigree's Tommy Gunn was one of the best. Much forgotten nowadays because of the popularity of Palitoy's Action Man.

By the time morning came, all our presents were laid out in our room and we'd fly out of bed at about 7am to open them all. Afterward, we'd rush into our mum and dad's bedroom to tell them what we'd got without realising that they'd actually bought them all.

There are a few things that I remember getting for Christmas 1969 including Beano and Dandy annuals and a Walt Disney Diary for 1970 which I filled out carefully each day until about February. Other presents included board games, which were very popular, and allsorts of

A much sought after Corgi Batmobile which came complete with firing rockets, flame exhaust and chain cutter. Every boy wanted to find one of these under the Christmas tree in the late 1960s.

other toys that we'd pestered our parents for on the lead up to Christmas. In the back of our minds, we must have realised that they were really Santa but it was far more fun believing in it all! Popular toys from 1969 that I remember included Spacehoppers, Hot Wheels racing tracks, Airfix models, anything to do with the Apollo mission, telescopes, annuals, toy soldiers and robots. We'd both give mum and dad their presents which, thinking about it now, weren't that exciting. Dad got some cigars or cigarettes (that mum had bought us to give him) or some Old Spice and mum got some chocolates. Gran always got hankies with her initials on them or Devon Violet bath salts. The kids definitely had the best deal!

One we were up, we'd be watching cartoons on the telly while mum would be preparing Christmas dinner. The whole day revolved around opening presents, Christmas dinner and watching the telly. Afternoons were spent trying out our new presents. One year I got a blue scooter and spent hours going up and down the street. Another

The Dinky toys that every boy wanted for Christmas including Battle of
Britain aeroplanes, a wonderful fire engine and vehicles from Joe 90.

time we had a pair of adjustable roller skates (they fitted any size) and when we went to try them out on the street, everyone had a pair!

Christmas dinner consisted of chicken or turkey with roast potatoes, carrots, stuffing and gravy. Mum would always make a currant Christmas pudding for afters which we'd have with custard. Inside the pudding, were coins, normally sixpences, and good luck charms. Afterwards, we'd pull our crackers. One year, we had special Flintstones crackers which contained Wade Whimsie versions of comical characters including a sabre-toothed tiger, a brontosaurus and one of Dino. When we got back to school, all the kids had them.

Once Boxing Day came around, it almost seemed a shame that all the build up to Christmas was over and we'd have to wait another year for another one. There was still all that Christmas food to eat and great programmes on the telly to watch but as the year drew on, suddenly the thought that we'd soon be back at school ruined everything. The decorations would stay up just long enough for us going back to school. We both always wanted to keep them up longer. Once they were taken down, the front room and our bedroom all looked very bare.

For me, some of our best times and best Christmases all took place in the 1960s. It was certainly a wonderful time to be a kid!

Some of the excellent toys that were available from Corgi in 1964 including a Mini, a Commer Milk Float and a London double-decker bus.